The
Runner
and the
Path

The
Runner
and the
Path

An Athlete's Quest for Meaning
in Postmodern Corporate America

DEAN OTTATI

BREAKAWAY BOOKS
HALCOTTSVILLE, NEW YORK
2008

The Runner and the Path © 2002 by Dean Ottati
Firat paperback edition 2008

ISBN: 978-1-891369-82-7
LIBRARY OF CONGRESS CONTROL NUMBER: 2001095145

Published by Breakaway Books
P.O. Box 24
Halcottsville, NY 12438
(800) 548-4348
www.breakawaybooks.com

FIRST PAPERBACK EDITION

For Zach,
because I never knew what my
dad was up to
when he had that
faraway look in his eyes.

ACKNOWLEDGMENTS

My deepest appreciation to:

Marc Liotta—mystic, mentor, friend, and inspiration.

My dad, who planted seeds that he never got to see grow.

My mom, who ensured that they could.

The Diablo Road Runners, and the rest of my family and friends; you are what make it a rich experience.

The Reverend Molly Darling, who, after reading the first draft, insisted on the radical notion that I write an outline, and then sat down with me to do it.

George Beinhorn, for your wonderfully sensitive editing hand.

Garth Battista of Breakaway Books, for taking a chance on an unknown writer—may the whole world catch your infectious enthusiasm.

Chris Ottati, my lifelong love, for encouraging me to follow every dream I ever held. May everyone be blessed with the support of someone like you.

Introduction

"Sit as little as possible. Give no credence to any thought that was not born outdoors, while one moved about freely—in which the muscles are not celebrating a feast too." —Nietzsche

I didn't start running to meet mystics, sages, and philosophers. I started running for the most common of reasons: to get back in shape. In January 1984, two years out of college, I had ballooned to my Jupiter weight of 195 pounds. In six short years, I had evolved from the captain of my high school swim team, working out five hours a day, six days a week, and harboring secret Olympic aspirations, to a couch potato carrying thirty extraneous pounds.

Nine months before we would marry, Chris, my fiancée, suggested I try running to trim the unwelcome pounds. Chris, an exercise physiologist by training, was the first of many running sages I'd encounter. Though I held dim views of running, I was willing to give it a try.

Until that time, I'd thought of running as a means of catching buses and outspeeding meter maids. Running was the body's natural response to fear, not to be engaged in for reasons aside from self-preservation. But love being the power it is, Chris and I ventured out to buy my first pair of running shoes the very day she suggested it. We then immediately ran a mile together, during which my thighs coughed and sputtered. The next morning, I had to walk downstairs facing backward. But I kept at it, and each week we added a half mile to the daily run, until we reached three miles a day.

After that, we continued to pile on the mileage, but we throttled back our schedule from six to just five days a week. Three months into the program, I had what I consider my first mystical run. Everything flowed as if I'd moved a little closer to the Source, tasting a small, satisfying sip from life's wellspring. I felt that I could run forever. I was hooked, and when Chris and I took our vows in September, I'd lost thirty pounds.

I had also become a runner. But this book isn't a how-to for losing weight, running a marathon, or getting faster. There are plenty of books to help with those endeavors. This book is about what's left when weight loss and competition cease to matter, and only the running remains.

For the first ten years I ran with Chris or with our two dogs, or I ran alone. I learned the many lessons of a regular running routine. I learned that in spite of my expectations, running has its own seasons and rhythms. Many times, I hit the pavement eager to run, only to discover that I felt drained, the body not ready at all. The spirit was willing, but the flesh was weak. Other times, I plea-bargained—*If I run twenty minutes, I can turn around and go home*—only to find that the run became a grand experience, an hour and a half of joy. Other times, the situation changed midrun.

I learned that the accomplishments I treasured most were the ones I had to work hard for, not those that came easily or naturally. Running a marathon is a great achievement not because of the 26.2 miles covered on a given day, but because of the many long Sunday training runs, and all the sacrifices made to bring me to the starting line with a real chance of finishing. Discipline can be both a means and an end.

Sometimes, I experienced the much-discussed runner's high, and I learned in the process that our limits are indeed far beyond where we imagine they are. But I've also hit the wall and discovered that the limits can be all too real. I learned, too, that a healthy activity like running can turn into a disastrous obsession. More than once, I ran when I should have rested, and got sick or injured. It takes experience to make out your own internal rhythms and accept them, to know that it's easy sometimes, and sometimes it's hard, and when the drill sergeant in your head tries to take over, you should ignore him. As I learned these lessons, the miles and the years piled up, their weight and presence becoming a body of work that provided context and meaning for my life.

Over time, the discipline of running became the yardstick against which other aspects of life were measured. As with running, relationships have seasons, too, and bad days that give way to good ones. As with running, the disappointment of a promotion passed by reveals itself to be the universe gathering energy for a greater swell of opportunity. And as with running, thoughts and moods that seem so vital and so real give way to calmer sensibilities.

Discipline teaches faith. In the midst of bad times, there's the knowledge, born of experience, that the good times return—and that knowledge helps. And when they do, we know, too, not to take them for granted. The cycles turn, and we can never really know where we are within them. But the piece of us that runs in the hills each day knows on a deep, cellular level that events play out precisely as they should. The inner runner accepts this. At a given moment, despite the tumult swirling all around, a small part of us remains at peace.

These are powerful spiritual lessons. Running turns any open place into my chapel. The hour I spend each day as an ascetic, short of water and feeling the slight discomfort of genuine effort, provides me with the strength to know that I can live with less than the world would have me believe. These lessons are really just the foundation for greater learning, though. At some point, connections must be made across the fabric of community. The lessons of ten years of running must be shared, but they must also be tested and refined in the free market of ideas. I began to seek the company of others outside my immediate family.

"Running is a very intimate experience." Deb, another in a long line of running mystics I'd meet, explained this to me on a snowy Chicago morning. Our footfalls hushed by an inch of fresh powder, Deb continued: "I know more about a person after running with him once than I know about a person I've dated many times." I believe Deb is right; the effort of the activity cuts through social veneers, leaving more of the core individual exposed.

Marc, the mystic around whom much of this book is written, once put it like this: "It's really about a search for meaning in our lives. I don't want a new car, a bigger house, or a more prestigious job. You can have those. I want more meaning in my life. It's not a search for truth, because there's a connotation in the word that implies correctness. I don't even expect to be right. What I really want is more meaning." The first time Marc said it, we were running on a single-track dirt trail that wound in and out of a beautiful green canyon that was alive with spring blossoms.

"Marc," I said, "this, right now, is what provides meaning for me. Our runs sustain me through the difficult times. When things get out of control, I think of our runs together.

They keep me sane."

"Yes," he replied. "There's something about being in nature, and experiencing a slight oxygen debt, and philosophizing about life. There's a German word, *Gemütlichkeit*, that means the experience of eating and drinking and socializing with loved ones. It isn't only eating or drinking or socializing—it's all three. It must be all three. When they come together, it has meaning. Our running together in beautiful places and contemplating the infinite is like that. It's all three things together—nature, effort, and philosophy—that give it meaning."

There's an aspect of the running experience I simply can't capture with my pen; nonetheless, I can't let it pass unmentioned. It's the good humor of the people I write about. It's beyond my ability to describe what it's like to run while I'm doubling over with laughter. I can't capture the feeling, or even the dialogue. In the end, it's just plain fun—a joy and a soaring liberation—to run with and know these people. I'm humbled by their courage and their wisdom in the face of daily life. It's been a privilege to spend time with them.

All the stories on these pages are true, though I'm presenting them somewhat out of order. Also, I've reshaped them to serve a point. Life seldom unfolds in conveniently sequential fashion. I've glossed over needlessly complicated details that might require long, boring explanations. But I've tried to be honest.

Sometimes, I've put my best foot forward—pun intended —but I've also avoided concealing the embarrassing blisters on that foot. And I've tried, where possible, to credit the giants who've inspired me, by quoting their works.

Even on a solitary running path, you never really run alone. The conversations and trails described here are mostly real, though I never take notes while I'm running. I've combined some of the stories and people into a single run, with a single person, although they're actually composites of weeks and months of conversations with several people. I've also changed some of the names and defining characteristics to protect the individual's privacy. But the running itself remains a very real, living human experience, and a very delightful way to travel the path we call life.

1

Running With Marc

"I went to the woods because I wished to live deliberately, to front only the essential facts of life, and see if I could not learn what it had to teach, and not, when I come to die, discover that I had not lived. I did not wish to practice resignation, unless it was quite necessary. I wanted to live deep and suck out all the marrow of life, to live so sturdily and Spartan-like as to put to rout all that was not life, to cut a broad swath and shave close, to drive life into a corner and reduce it to its lowest terms, and, if it proved to be mean, why then to get the whole and genuine meanness of it, and publish its meanness to the world; or if it were sublime, to know it by experience, and be able to give a true account of it in my next excursion." —Henry David Thoreau, *Walden*

The long fingers of El Niño were groping into June. On my way to meet the running club, I turned the windshield wipers to high and gave my arm another idle scratch. A pink, dry spot was all that remained of the poison oak I'd contracted three weeks earlier while running muddy trails with Marc. During the run, I slipped on a steep hill and ended up swimming in the venomous bushes bordering the trail. Now, I felt anxious. I'd just finished my second course of prednisone this year— the doctor had just laughed when I'd come into her office this last time. Leaving the house, Chris had suggested that I ignore Marc's enticements and run a different route. Poison oak interfered with everything, from sleep to hugging Zach, my one-year-old son. The itch impacted others. I had responsibilities. Maybe so, but it's never easy to ignore Marc.

It "never" rains in June in Walnut Creek, California, where I live. Our running routes are drawn well in advance; unfortunately, the weather never bothers to consult the schedule. The evening's run would be an out-and-back up a wide dirt trail into Castle Rock Canyon, a notorious poison oak mecca— Castle Rock is where all the world's poison oak plants gather to grab a trophy runner at least once in their lifetime. My mind wandered to the many alternate routes through suburban streets that we could run, smooth, clean, paved roads lined with ryegrass, where the biggest threat is an occasional rosebush raised with the good manners to post bright warning flowers. *Why do I do this? I can turn around and go home. I don't like running in the rain.* Even as the whiny thoughts emerged, they felt uncomfortably wrong.

When I arrived at the base of the canyon, five cars were waiting. I spotted Marc's van with its CLOSET MAGICIAN sign, reflecting the business he'd started eighteen years ago after dropping out of corporate America. "You can never go broke

in this business," Marc once quipped. "The first thing suburban housewives want when they wake up and realize they're
leading unfulfilled lives is to straighten their closets. It never
works, but it keeps me going." Seeing the van, I knew I was
in trouble—Marc was here, and responsibilities and health be
damned, there was no doubt where we'd be running tonight.

A run with Marc is as uplifting as any sermon, as inspiring as
the voyage of brave Ulysses. Tonight, we'd slay the Hydra of
poison oak, and we'd emerge stronger and smarter. Running
with Marc sustained me; it was an opportunity I could never
pass up. I pulled into the muddy lot and five car windows rolled
down and five faces stared out. Barbara was the first to speak.

"We all want to do the Heather Farms loop, but Marc wants
to stay here." I spotted Marc emerging from behind the van,
lord and master of his closet empire, looking like a crinkle-eyed
cross between Merlin and Charlton Heston's Moses in *The Ten
Commandments*, preparing to lead us to the Promised Land.
His mane of thick salt-and-pepper hair glistened in the mist.
"We've got to run here," Marc said, tapping a brown puddle
sonata with a Nike-clad toe. "You must fight the postmodern
experience! You'll have the time of your life!" His youthful
enthusiasm belied his fifty-four years.

"You're the tiebreaker, Dean," Barbara said.

How is it, I wondered, *that five grown adults, born and
raised in this great democratic land, feel it's a tie when only Marc
votes against them? And why am I the tiebreaker?* "Come on,

Barbara, I've never been able to say no to Marc," I said, glancing at my healing arm as Marc continued his muddy jig, splattering dirt on his thin, muscular calves. I stepped out of the car and pulled on the powder blue UCLA baseball cap I wear in the rain. "Marc says we'll have the time of our lives. I should argue?"

As the seven of us started up the canyon, I veered to the middle of what had once been a trail but was now a muddy reddish brown skating rink. We climbed and slipped, two steps forward, one step back, literally. At this rate, the seven-mile run would take two hours. With three pounds of wet clay clinging to the bottom of each shoe, I scuffed at every passing rock to lighten the load for a few steps. Regardless, I felt giddy and light as a kid sneaking out after dark, tasting the smell of adventure. The slow pace left breath for laughter. After several tough meetings earlier in the day, it felt good to let go. I led the group to the first of fourteen stream crossings, then slowed and settled in next to Marc.

"All right, I'll bite. What the hell is 'the postmodern experience'? And why must we fight it?"

"The postmodern experience is about removing ourselves from actual experience," Marc said. "It's about watching sports on TV instead of participating. It's about having love affairs on the Internet instead of real, intimate contact. It's about having a drink instead of confronting the issues. It's about running on treadmills instead of in the rain. Great stuff happens! Good or bad, we mustn't insulate ourselves from it—we must experience it."

My right foot hit the next stream. The water parted and for a brief miraculous instant the foot remained dry. Neurons dispatched a message to my brain, claiming victory over the waters. But as the message emerged to the forechamber of consciousness, a cold shock of water hit my foot. Too late, the brain sent a high-step command. There would be no dry-foot miracles tonight. I congratulated myself for donning old shoes.

"You're saying that getting our feet wet is part of the visceral experience of running, and instead of talking about wet feet, we should feel wet feet?"

"That's right." Marc winked.

"My wet sock is part of a great rebellion against the postmodern experience?"

"Yes! Each wet sock is a stinking foot soldier in the war against postmodernism." Marc laughed, then turned serious. "Thoreau wrote a beautiful passage about how you must drive life into a corner and suck the marrow from the bone."

I loved listening to Marc on his soapbox, to the extent that I often dreamed up questions to prime the fountain, as the other club runners often did. No subject was taboo or beyond reach. Philosophy, politics, religion, sex, abortion, business, political correctness, any topic made good fodder for Marc's impromptu ramblings. At such times, running turned into flight. The miles melted away, and I was left more energized than when we started.

"But what does that mean, driving life into a corner?" I said.

"It means you can't stop the juggernaut of time—it's relentless. You must get as much as you can out of each moment. Live life directly. Don't remove yourself from experience. Make love on the dining room table! Howl at the moon! Run muddy trails in the rain!" He smiled and turned, looking deeply into my eyes, serious. Speaking softly, he said, "Watch these people. Look at how animated they are."

We ran in silence for a while. Marc was right. A giddiness had taken hold of the group. At the next stream, Barbara slammed a foot in the water, splashing Jay. At the next crossing, Jay retaliated by dipping a hand in the stream and splashing Barbara. Others joined in the battle, and each crossing brought an escalation of technique, culminating in Jay's removing Barbara's hat, filling it with water, and slapping it on her head. We laughed harder than on any of our previous runs.

The trail narrowed to a single track, and I could hear the poison oak tentacles straining to reach us, as if struggling to share some nasty plant nectar. I slipped, and my legs grazed a patch of the pestiferous stuff. In a day or two, I'd be enjoying plenty of direct, itchy, oozing life experience. For no reason, rather than curse my fate, I laughed and glanced at Marc. "Let's get you rinsed off," he said sympathetically.

Sitting in the cold stream, scrubbing the leg with dirt, I

turned to Marc and said, "It's cold and wet. We all wanted to run another route. Why are we having such a good time?"

Marc said, "Thoreau also wrote 'The mass of men lead lives of quiet desperation.' As remedy, he encouraged people to 'Simplify, simplify, simplify.' What could be simpler than running in the rain?"

I recoiled from the quote on quiet desperation, pushing it out of my mind before thoughts could form. I said, "Yes, but Thoreau had it easy, in a way." I stood and we resumed squishing down the trail. "He was single. He lived in a cabin in the woods. We live in the suburbs. We have families, mortgages, and responsibilities."

Marc said, "Did you know that Thoreau's first draft of that famous sentence was: 'A stereotype but unconscious despair is concealed under what are called the amusements of mankind.' What a load of psychobabble! Thank God for keeping that train wreck of a sentence out of the ditch. The 'simple cabin' stuff is overrated, too. Did you ever visit Walden?"

"No."

"Thoreau lived a mile from where he grew up. He had visitors at the cabin all the time. He was never isolated. His separation was symbolic, not real. Thoreau said he was determined to 'move away from public opinion, from government, from religion, from education, from society.' He said he was 'determined to meet myself face to face.' He didn't have to go very far to do those things. Today, everyone who makes a few bucks wants to think of himself as self-sufficient and independent and self-made. It's a bunch of bull. Thoreau was never deluded that way. He understood his reliance on others."

"Okay, I surrender," I said. "He didn't move far. But that doesn't explain why this run is so much fun."

"Ahhh," Marc said, "that's because, for this moment in the rain, we're distancing ourselves from the postmodern experience and coming back in contact with the experience of our lives. You probably spent the drive over here thinking of all the reasons you shouldn't run tonight. Am I right?"

"Yes," I confessed.

"Do you ever wonder why you spend your time doing that? It's because you've gotten the idea that you don't like running in the rain. The reality is, you do like running in the rain, because it's pure visceral joy and sensual pleasure. People only think they don't like it, but it's fun. Give the credit to the negative ions that are being stirred up by the rain, or whatever—it doesn't matter. I bet you'd be hard pressed to remember a single time you didn't enjoy running in the rain."

"Are you saying the postmodern experience is about the difference between an idea about something and the actuality of it?"

"Yes! That's what I'm saying." Marc smiled. "When we know our actual experience as it really is, and not just as we think it is or should be, we meet the truth. We lead the examined life, and for a little while, at least, we aren't desperate."

Just as in every movie with themes of Native American mysticism, an eagle screeched overhead, flying west to east— a powerful sign. The evening crackled with currents of revelation. I'd returned a little closer to myself.

"Marc, this is kind of a reverse example, but I think the postmodern experience explains the resurgent popularity of cigar smoking."

"How's that?"

"Well," I hesitated, "I can't believe that many people actually enjoy the damn things. They're foul smelling, and they make you dizzy and sick. At least, that's my experience, and I don't think I'm alone. But I can believe lots of people *think* they enjoy a good cigar, or they enjoy the image they think cigar smoking projects."

"Yes, that's it. It's the Disneyland effect—where the theme-park village is more Swiss than Switzerland. We think we like these things, but the experience is really quite hollow."

The others didn't hear Marc's sermon. Perhaps they didn't need it. But for all of us, that evening's run would remain the standard against which all future club runs would be measured.

I had a final question. "Did you stay up all night brushing up on Thoreau?"

"Last time I read it was thirty-five years ago. The man didn't just put ink scratches on paper. He caught the wind that blows from the center of the universe. He raised the level of what it means to be human. When you encounter such a thing, it changes you. You don't easily forget it." Back in the parking lot, Marc wrapped a towel around his waist and stripped out of his running shorts, then rummaged in the van for a gallon jug of water, which he poured over himself to rinse off the sweat and mud. Laughing, he pulled on a pair of navy blue fuzzy sweats and quipped, "Portable locker room!"

"Why so formal?" I said.

"I've heading over to The Bird to quote a job."

"The Bird?"

"Yeah, Blackhawk," he said, referring to an exclusive gated community. "The place where unfulfilled suburbanites look to actualize their dreams with their parents' money." Marc jumped behind the steering wheel, gave his trademark friendly smile, and drove into the night.

On the way home, body heat radiated through my wet clothes, steaming the windows, as I reflected on our conversation. I'd always shied away from Thoreau's phrase "a life of quiet desperation," believing it meant other people's lives. I had tried to push it away tonight, but as elated as I felt, I couldn't ignore my own secret, long-nourished pangs of desperation.

Yet it made little sense, so I responded as a trained businessman, drawing up a mental checklist and ticking off the items. I was happily married. I had a beautiful son. I had my health. I ran regularly. The economy was good. I lived in a modest house, carefully selected to reduce mortgage burden. I had no other debts. I lived in a beautiful area. What could possibly be wrong?

These pangs of desperation are the self-indulgent musings of a privileged little boy, I thought. *They can't be real. Or can they?* I continued to tick off the items on my mental checklist. I had a good job that paid well. I enjoyed a short commute. If only my customers would stop being so unreasonable! The words bucked in my head: *If only.* Now we were getting somewhere, and I knew where to begin the soul-searching.

Beginnings, like endings, are hard to pin down. Did it begin on the drive home that night? Or did it begin the moment Marc quoted Thoreau's famous words? I could argue that it had begun the moment I first shook Marc's hand, or when I first laced up a pair of running shoes. I could make a compelling case that the roots were planted in swimming, where I'd learned to love working out. Or I could make an equally compelling argument that it had begun when my parents, both swimmers, transmitted their love of the sport to me.

Each argument was correct, but to hold on to any of them would be to separate and elevate it above the rest. All of those antecedent events were required. I prefer not to think of that evening's run as a beginning, but as a change in velocity. The run and the rainy night's conversation reinvigorated my journey of self-discovery.

Sixteen years before, when I graduated from college, I hadn't seen how deeply the yearning to understand had sunk its taproot into me. Instead, I allowed myself to be distracted. I let money, career, status, and all the trappings of success become more important than the search for meaning. Now, feeling the tingling quiet desperation of which Thoreau spoke, I could no longer ignore those yearnings. They were deep within me, and I had to attend to them.

It wasn't that I'd suddenly decided to take up the search for meaning. Stating it that way would minimize the search by exposing it to a host of confused notions about what really happened. The yearning that waited quietly in the background for sixteen years was infinitely larger and more patient than I was. I was merely ready to reacknowledge it. This deep yearning, this quest for meaning, this search, is bigger than I am, bigger than any words. I can't define it; the most true thing I can say about it is that the search for meaning decided to take me. I had no real choice in the matter.

Early in the evening, Marc had encouraged me to fight the postmodern experience. Now I found myself thinking that life would be perfect *if only* my customers were more reasonable. The *if-onlys* in our lives are signals, spelling out that we believe our lives should be different than they are. I'd soon find myself stumbling over many *if-onlys*. My search would begin by examining the *if-onlys* in detail.

2

Running With Doug

"The trouble with the rat race is that even if you win, you're still a rat." —Lily Tomlin

Life is paradox. When it comes to politics, Doug and I couldn't be farther apart, but I think a world filled with people like Doug would be a pretty good place to live. Doug and I had been through the wars together. We'd forged our relationship during seven major contract negotiations with tens of millions of dollars hanging in the balance. The pinnacle achievement of our careers had come when, two and a half years earlier, nine days before Christmas, we received a request for proposal for a contract to build a digital cellular network in Atlanta and Sacramento. We were given a week to respond.

Doug and I suspected that the customer, SkyReach, had set a tight Christmas deadline as a sly bargaining tactic, to ensure a hasty decision on our part. If so, it worked. While the rest of the staff left for the holidays, the burden fell on Doug and me, at the time relatively junior members of the RadioGear team. Nearing the stroke of midnight, three days before the deadline, we arrived at an epiphany about how to win the contract. Two months later, we had conceived, negotiated, and closed a seventy-million-dollar deal. I tell people that if World War III broke out, Doug would jump in my foxhole. Truly, it works both ways—I can think of nobody with whom I'd rather enter a problematic customer negotiation, because I can always count on Doug.

His primary sport isn't running, but he consents to run when we get together, and he's fit enough to run, while I'm not inclined or fit enough to move indoors for his Lifecycle, Stairmaster, and weight workouts.

On an early morning before work, we jogged along the Newport Bay Estuary in Southern California. We were negotiating retributions with SkyReach, making amends for the many times the SkyReach RadioGear networks had crashed, bringing phone service down in seven major cites. The objective was to buy time for RadioGear's software development teams, which were working to address the network availability troubles. Fixing the root cause of the problems—poor software quality—just wasn't immediately feasible.

Our time had run out. SkyReach had experienced more than 180 system failures of varying impact over the preceding nine months, and they were understandably fed up. They no longer were looking for retribution; they wanted a permanent solution. After spending two days reviewing statistics on the cost differential of managing and maintaining RadioGear networks versus its competitors', Doug and I had just about reached breaking point. We'd listened to endless emotionally charged tales of how their cell-site technicians crossed hill and dale in darkest night to bring out-of-service cell sites online, armed only with their wits and Swiss army knives. We felt trapped. Deep down we agreed with SkyReach, and software development, the real source of the problems, was beyond our control.

We ran the first quarter mile in silence, loosening our morning legs. We settled into a running rhythm, and after a few minutes Doug said, "I keep thinking of the story you told about the question your professor asked in business school."

"Which one?"

"In the sales class, where he asked if anyone had ever tried selling an inferior product."

A white crane rose in the air and canted to the right, leaving two sets of concentric rings in the shallow water. I said, "I remember him asking the question, and I remember thinking, *I'll never be in sales, and I'll certainly never put myself in the position of selling an inferior product.* And now, here we are. What's the old expression? 'You mock that which you are to become.'"

We wound along the sinuous arms of the estuary. Doug

said, "Now you know what it feels like, and your professor was right. We always go into these negotiations hanging our heads, apologizing for our products, and buying time for development to fix the problems, but they never do. We've done this for three and a half years, and here's what I don't get. You graduated first in your class from the number one business school in the country. You live in the start-up capital of the world. You could go do anything you want. Why do you continue to put up with it?"

I glanced at the sky. Patches of blue appeared and disappeared in the shifting clouds as the morning marine layer began to break up. Mansions lined the cliffs on our right, their two-story, floor-to-ceiling windows looking out over shallows of green and brown pussy willows set in a blue mix of salt and fresh water. I thought of my classmates who'd started Garden.com and made fortunes. I thought of the Silicon Valley entrepreneurs who'd made millions in stock options, while I kept putting myself in these uncomfortable situations. A twinge of envy arose, but in a few seconds it passed.

I smiled, recalling a question a classmate of mine at Kellogg Graduate School of Management had asked, similar to Doug's. "Dean," she said, "how does it feel to graduate from a top business school, at just the right time, only to miss out on the greatest period of wealth creation in all of human history?" Molly, who during this same period left her high-paying management consulting job to become an Episcopal priest, delights in a good torment.

I answered Doug, "Yes, I think about all the people getting rich starting dotcoms, and I wonder why I'm not doing it. I guess there are lots of reasons. I like not having to commute. I like going home for lunch. You know how hard we work, so you'll understand when I say this. I don't want to spend the next years of my life completely devoted to the job. I just can't do it. At times, we put in lots of hours, but there's also an ease that comes with knowing the business. And I can't explain why, but I have the overwhelming feeling that there's something I need to learn in this job, and that I haven't quite learned it yet."

"What do you mean?"

"Let me put it like this. A few years ago, Chris and I took a scuba vacation in Belize. We'd go for a run every morning, then we'd sit on the beach until our first dive. And every morning, a man dressed in rumpled clothes and wearing a two-day stubble would come by and sell us a newspaper. I have no idea how he managed to have a two-day stubble every day, but I could tell from his accent that he came from New York. We talked, and over the week I discovered that he'd been a junk bond trader on Wall Street during the 1980s, and that he'd made and lost a megafortune. He'd salvaged enough to buy a house in Belize and retire. He was living off his remaining investments, and he sold newspapers for something to do. He said he felt it was time to go back to the States. Toward the end of our vacation, I asked him, 'Here you are, living the American dream. You've retired on the beach in paradise, and now you want to return. Why?' He gave a sad, knowing smile and said, 'It turns out, wherever you go, you bring your karma with you,' and he walked away. I never saw him again, but I think about him often."

"What do you think he meant?" Doug said.

"I think he saw a recurring pattern in his life, and he'd learned that running away to the beach didn't make it go away. He concluded that the problems he was trying to run away from lay within himself."

"But what does that have to do with us?"

"Bear with me. I don't love my job, and I'm not sure why. Here we are, you and I. We're midlevel managers who've had the rare opportunity to negotiate deals worth millions. Two and a half years ago, we spent every night for a week in our 'war room' just before Christmas, and we won a contract worth seventy million dollars. How many people get to do a deal that size in any business? In our company, we're the only ones at our level who've done it. Most of our superiors have never come close to closing a deal that big. It's unheard of, yet here we are, and it's exciting. But the job still pisses me off a lot of the time, and I think I need to stick it out until I understand why it pisses me off."

Doug said, "That's because we've been doing it for so long,

and it never seems to get better. Whatever we do, it's never enough. The customers complain, and they never mention the good things we do. It borders on abuse. Yet the software keeps coming out with bugs, and there are just so many apologies you can offer. After a while it begins to wear on you. The company has got to start delivering, or you and I should think about moving on. . . . I think maybe it's time to move on."

I glanced up to see an endangered osprey in profile, its crooked beak silhouetted against the sky, its black wings folded over its white body, watching us from a tree branch. For reasons I couldn't understand, I had the feeling it was a wise old bird.

I tried a different approach. I said, "This job is all about relationships: the relationship to our customers, and the relationship to the 'mother ship' in Chicago. And we sit in the middle, trying to align the two. I get frustrated when we can't get the ends of the relationship to go where we want them to. But why do I get frustrated, if I'm doing the best I can?"

Without realizing it, we had picked up the pace, and I slowed to catch my breath. "I think all of life is about relationships—relationships with customers, with family, with ourselves. Everything is relationships, and I won't be able to get any relationship right until I can get this one right. This is the one that's on the front burner.

"When I took the job, I'd call JP"—he was a mentor of

Doug's and mine—"and cry on his shoulder about how I was being beaten up by SkyReach. I once told him I thought I needed to develop a thicker skin, and do you know what he said? He said, 'You get upset because you care. You don't want to lose that quality. If you develop a thicker skin when you're dealing with SkyReach, you'll bring it home with you, and it won't work.' Of course, JP went on to say that I'd married above my station, and that if I stopped caring at home Chris would leave me, and I'd spend my life sitting in my underwear crying about it. But his point was valid. You can't compartmentalize your life, no matter how much you try. Work and home aren't separable. Somehow, the way you treat one relationship will always carry over to the way you handle the others."

"Yeah," Doug said. "That sounds like JP. I know how he is. But where do you draw the line? When do you just say 'Enough is enough'?"

"Every relationship is a paradox. In a way, relationships are like running. It takes commitment and discipline to get through the hard times and make running a regular part of your life. Sometimes, it's really just too much, and you have to stop if you want to avoid getting injured. The hard part is knowing when to stick it out and when to let go.

"I think I have to stick with this job because it's the second time I've been the go-between for two large groups that didn't trust one another. I never told you about this. My last job before I decided to go to graduate school was filled with the same hostility, deceit, and anger. So this is my second time around."

"You feel your karma is following you?" Doug said.

"Yes. There's something about my relationship to work, and about dealing with angry people, that I need to learn."

"What do you think it is?"

"I'm not sure, but I think it has something to do with developing a thinner skin and becoming more sensitive, not more hardened. I know that runs contrary to the usual advice."

We had climbed out of the estuary and made the turn back toward the hotel. Now we had some real work ahead of us.

3

Running With Richard

"On the twelfth hole our drive was into the wind, down a narrow fairway that dog-legged to the right. Familiar images of disaster came back to haunt me as I took my stance. I sliced the drive and the sea breeze carried it into the rough. Shivas walked along beside me up the fairway, and asked me what I was thinking. I told him about the awful thoughts. 'They'll pass,' he said, 'if ye daena' fight 'em. Come back to where'er ye were a minute ago. Wait 'em oot.' Those words were a great help—not only for the rest of the round but for my life ever since. The admonition to 'wait 'em oot' was one of those sayings that came back to haunt me."
—Michael Murphy, *Golf in the Kingdom*

Every sport produces its mystics and philosophers, convinced that their particular discipline best enables its practitioners to transcend pedestrian consciousness and experience a facet of ultimate Truth. And you can't really blame them. It's easy to feel Yin fading into Yang in the breath of the straining runner, to imagine the Buddha seated peacefully at the hub of the cyclist's wheel, to hear Perfection when the tennis ball meets the sweet spot on the racket, or to watch the Hand of Grace guide the golf ball on a magic carpet from trap to pin.

In the moment of "Ahhh" before the logical mind starts analyzing what happened, evaluating the results, and making plans to make it happen again, sport really does remove the veil and allow us to glimpse a greater perfection at work around and within us. The "Ahhh" experience explains why a golfer can shoot just one good stroke in eighteen holes and still look forward to playing again. Loving the experience, rather than the results, also explains why a sport's lesser practitioners are often the ones who learn its subtle truths.

Richard is such a practitioner. An average golfer who deeply loves the game, he's a little bit distrustful of the sport's cigar-smoking, meat-eating, back-scratching, deal-making good-old-boy side. And he likes people to know he's different.

I met Richard during a Shriner charity golfing event. He was wearing Scots plaid knickers, a billowy hat, blinding white socks, and saddle shoes. At six-foot-three and 185 pounds, with carrot red hair, he stood out in a crowd renowned for its bad outfits. But in contrast with his loud appearance, Richard's nonconformity masked a quiet thoughtfulness.

As we set out for the first tee in our cart, Richard waxed eloquent about how, if God had intended golfers to ride,

He'd have given them two gloves instead of one. By the third tee, he'd convinced me that in the natural order of things, our rightful place demanded that we walk. Richard told me that Ben Hogan, Arnold Palmer, and Jack Nicklaus all walked, not because the rules of professional golfing required it, but because it was impossible to feel the rhythms of the game otherwise. To ride was to be disconnected from the greater forces working within the game. So we ditched our cart, and for the rest of the day we walked, not only to play golf but to be at one with golf. Tapping straight into the greater golf cosmos, we shot a ninety-five and finished dead last. Such is the chuckling good humor of golf's gods.

Several months later, I saw Richard again. I was running on the beach in Del Mar, during a business trip to Southern California, and I was thinking about life, when Richard pulled even, wearing shorts imprinted with tiny putting greens and a T-shirt that said LIVE TO GOLF, GOLF TO LIVE.

"How are you doing?" he asked, dropping into my pace.

"Been a little blue," I said. "Chris and I had another fight about picking up the house before the cleaning people come. It pisses me off. She gets so worked up about straightening the house for the people we pay good money to come clean the place. That's what we're paying them for! It got ugly. It's happening more and more, and the more we try to talk about it, the worse it gets. We wind up lying in bed, not talking and not sleeping. At times like that, I just want to leave and never come back."

Richard said, "I just read *Golf in the Kingdom* by Michael Murphy. There's a great passage that might help you. The author is golfing with his mystical teacher, Shivas Irons. He's having bad thoughts about all the mistakes he might make, and his golf game is beginning to reflect his thinking. So he asks Shivas what to do about the bad thoughts, and Shivas says with his Scottish accent, 'They'll pass, if you wait 'em oot.'"

Six gray sandpipers turned in unison and sprinted quick-legged into the receding waves, bobbing double-time for sand crabs, then turned again in retreat before the ensuing wave. Our path wove to avoid the incoming water, waffled shoe prints disappearing behind us. "So how does this sage advice relate to my marriage woes?" I asked.

"Do you remember when we last golfed, I was explaining how the Bible says that God is the creator, and that man is created in God's image, so that means we're creators too?"

"Yes."

"Well, if you remember, I was studying *A Course in Miracles* at the time, and an underlying premise of the Course is that our thoughts create our reality. At the time, I thought it meant that we need to control our thoughts, and I spent a whole day trying to control everything that popped into my head. I couldn't do it. I realized it's just not the human condition, or at least not my condition, to continually censor my thoughts. But it frustrated me."

"So that explains how we could be dialed into the golf gods and shoot a ninety-five. Must have had the wrong number." I said.

"Yes, that's why! When I read that passage in *Golf in the Kingdom*, the proverbial lightning bolt hit me. Our thoughts and our emotions are like waves on the ocean," he said, pointing to the sea, where surfers rose and fell, their wet suits glistening like seal skin, and spray, backlit by the afternoon sun, fanned off the cresting blue-green waves.

"They keep coming, but from what source I don't know. They just do. It's our choice which thoughts we choose to ride to the beach. Which thoughts and emotions, in other words, we'll latch onto and identify with, and which ones we'll let pass, knowing that others are coming. Shivas Irons says, 'They'll pass, if ye daena' fight 'em.' In other words, let the set of bad waves go by. There's always another set. If you choose not to ride them, they pass more quickly."

"I hear what you're saying, but what about principles, and standing up for what you believe in?"

"What do you mean?"

"Well, for example, we work our butts off so we can afford cleaning people. I come home, and I want to be with Chris and Zach. It doesn't make sense to spend our precious time straightening up." Piles of brown kelp blocked our way around a rocky point. Sand fleas, celebrating the ocean's bounty, flitted about the shining fronds. With his long, flowing strides, Richard navigated the point with ease, while I struggled with awkward, off-balance, crisscrossing steps.

"The trouble is," Richard said, compassion filling his deep blue eyes, "the bad thoughts and emotions feel so vital, so much like life and death, so real. We get pissed off. We swear. We contemplate divorce. We spend so much energy convincing ourselves that we're right, validating our point of view by selectively twisting the facts, persuading ourselves that no other alternatives could possibly exist. We become so attached to a particular thought that we mistake it for principle, for part of our core being. Yet these thoughts and feelings aren't us. They're not what we really think, or how we really feel. They're temporary, like passing waves. Still, the force of the water pushes us."

Two surfers, paddling hard, caught a medium wave while a dozen others waited, staring out to sea. The wave closed out quickly before the two could stand, washing their boards to shore. "I remember you told me you'd married your soul mate. I also remember your saying your boy has serious eczema, asthma, and allergies. Has any of that changed?"

"Zach still has troubles, and they're life-threatening. But maybe I was wrong about the soul mate thing."

"How long have you been married?" Richard asked.

"Fourteen years."

"I'm afraid it's too late for you. After fourteen years, you usually don't make mistakes about the soul mate thing. It's your blessing and your curse, because she'll point out things about you that you could never find out on your own. She's pointing out one right now, only you haven't realized it." We ran quietly for a while, then Richard said, "Did you ever stop to consider that maybe Chris wants you to straighten up so that the cleaning people can spend more time focusing on the things that will help Zach's allergies, like ridding his room of dust mites? Do you really resent helping straighten up so much?"

At this point, three miles south of where I'd started my run, we turned and headed back. With the ocean on our left now, we hugged the high-water line, running on the moist, hard-packed sand to gain traction while trying to avoid getting our feet wet. Our path meandered in and out, guided by the ocean's whimsy.

"When you put it that way, I don't," I said.

Richard continued, "If Chris is a typical female, she probably wants to talk about Zach's health and the importance of keeping a clean house. She wants you to know how deeply she cares about Zach, and she wants you to understand how much of herself she sacrifices to keep him healthy. Having a one-year-old is a very isolating experience. When you add his medical condition, it's even more so. She needs you to understand her sacrifice and isolation. If you're a typical guy, you just want to fix the problem. You want to hire a cleaning person and be done with it. For Chris, straightening up before the cleaning person comes is a way to gain some measure of control over a situation where she has almost none. It's her way of helping make his situation just a little bit better. She knows she can't make Zach healthy, but she can try. Meanwhile, the needs of a toddler have completely over-whelmed her own needs. Her response is to ask for your help straightening up, so that you're working together on the major problem, connecting Chris back to the world from which she feels so isolated. You, being a typical guy, don't understand the need for communal experience as well as she does. If you can't fix it, it's out of your control, and you just want to move on. Zach places lots of demands on Chris, so you'll hire a cleaning person, problem solved. Women gener-ally don't work that way."

"We both want the best for Zach," I said. "You're talking about the whole *Men Are From Mars, Women Are From Venus* thing. Are we doomed to spend the rest of our days knowing fundamentally different communication styles and never connecting?" A sliver of desperation had crept into my voice.

"Zach is the common ground," Richard said. "You both love him and want what's best for him. You'll be fine. A wise man once told me that if you want to do what's best for your children, you should work on your relationship with your spouse."

We ran in silence for a while, instinctively veering to the right at the thunderclap of a large wave crashing near shore.

The ensuing rush of water pushed against the side of my left shoe and receded just as it reached the top of the sole where rubber met nylon mesh. My foot stayed dry. The beach shimmered before us in the sunlight, pebbles and shells rolling back toward the sea. In stride, we veered left again toward the water. After a few minutes, we reached the pier where I had started.

Ever a sucker for making a conversation come full circle, I looked at Richard and said, "What does the way Chris and I communicate have to do with Shivas Irons and the *Course in Miracles?*"

Richard turned toward me, his crow's-feet accentuated as he squinted in the afternoon sun. He gave me a mischievous elfin smile, silent, and began removing his shirt. I knew instantly what he was thinking. I sat and pulled off my shoes, careful not to get sand in them, rolled my socks in little balls, and stuffed them in the shoes. Richard tossed his clothes carelessly up the beach. Stripped to our running shorts, we looked at each other and sprinted to the sea, laughing. The cool water felt good against my heated skin. Thirty yards out, we dove under a breaking wave. I kept my eyes open as I entered the foamy blue-green world. I did a breaststroke pull and kick underwater to pull beyond the reach of the wave's grip. For a brief moment, I stopped struggling and lingered, buoyant between the ocean swells, enjoying the clean salt smell.

Richard's head bobbed to the surface five feet to my right. He shook the hair out of his face and let out a big "Ahhh!"

We paddled slowly out past the breakers. Seagulls patrolled the skies overhead. After a few minutes, Richard broke the silence. "I haven't forgotten your question. It's just that a good run calls for a reward. There's a lesson in the *Course* where you're supposed to ask yourself: *Would you rather be right, or would you rather be happy?* That lesson stayed with me a long time. What I think it means is—well, let's take your example. It takes lots of mental energy to be resentful about cleaning the house, and all it really does is alienate you from your soul mate. You're right, you shouldn't have to clean up before the cleaning people come. But you know what? Chris is right, too. If you straighten up before they arrive, the cleaning people will probably have more time to spend on the things that help Zach. Zach and Chris are the most important thing in the world to you, so why waste energy fighting something that helps them both? That energy might be better spent cleaning."

"Are you saying that if I always submit to Chris's whims, I'll wind up being happier?"

"No, of course not. If you always, as you put it, submit to Chris's whims, you'll just end up being resentful. You can't cling to the old mind-set and keep trying to be right, even while you help with the cleaning. If you're doing that, then nothing's really changed inside, where it counts. You and Chris need to talk about these things."

"Elaborate," I said, feeling suddenly serious.

"You need to continue to communicate, but usually the point of conflict is the absolute worst time to try to do so. Save the conversation for later. The times when we need our best communicating skills are usually when we've got the least amount of emotional resources to use them. We're too busy convincing ourselves we're right about the situation, and convincing the other person we're right. We aren't really accepting the situation for what it is. In your case, if you submit to Chris's whims, a piece of your energy will be splintered off. You'll be telling yourself you're right, that cleaning is a stupid activity, while at the same time you're spending energy doing the cleaning. You'll continue to fight yourself, squandering your energies every time the cleaning person comes. You'll have nothing left over for constructive communication, so don't even try. Save it for later. When things are calm, and there isn't as much inner turmoil, talk it over with Chris. I'm willing to bet you'll learn that you both really want the same thing, in this case, to help Zach. Your energies will be working together to build something, instead of working against each other to defend your separate positions."

"And as a result, we'll be happier together?" I asked.

"So the *Course in Miracles* and Shivas Irons would lead us to believe."

"Richard," I asked, "what is the miracle in the *Course in Miracles*?"

"It's not walking on water, if that's what you mean. The

Course defines a miracle as the point where an ancient hatred becomes a present love. In other words, it's a shift in perception from hatred for someone or something, to love. It's a change within ourselves, not a change in the outside world."

"That looks like a good wave. Should we bodysurf it?"

"Let it pass," Richard said. The breath of the ocean lifted us six feet off the sandy bottom and set us gently down. Brief seconds later, the wave closed out with a resounding clap—unridable, it would have dumped us to the ocean floor and held us under. Out beyond the surf, for a long time Richard and I rocked peacefully in the ocean's liquid arms. Surfers caught rides, some gliding in to the shore, others wiping out. Sunshine caressed our faces as we floated, happy to be alive, letting the waves pass.

Richard's advice proved prophetic. Soon after our conversation, Chris and I talked about the housecleaning. We discovered that neither of us liked having someone do the cleaning for us. Chris felt the cleaning people were doing a good job, but that they were too focused on finishing quickly to provide the extraordinary cleaning measures required to protect Zach. Often, if a food or environmental allergen can be eliminated from the environment, a child's body can "forget" that it is allergic and "outgrow" the allergy. The same is often true for adults.

Chris liked the idea of having more control of Zach's care, in however small measure, and I liked the idea of not paying someone to do something I'd have to redo, regardless. We enjoyed the luxury of hiring a baby-sitter once a month with the additional funds, and going out for dinner and a movie. Eliminating the cleaning service seemed contrary to what many families might think they'd want, but for us, it was right. It made me wonder how many other misguided assumptions we held about what we thought we wanted.

I didn't immediately grasp the more abstract portions of Richard's advice. His ideas had been clear, but I simply wasn't capable of hearing everything he said. We tend to see the world through tinted glasses, not realizing we're wearing them. It wasn't until I took off the glasses that I was able to examine Richard's words more closely. Meanwhile, I struggled to understand.

There's a popular idea in our culture nowadays that the thoughts we hold create our reality. Entire self-help industries have been built upon this notion. One variation on this theme was first propagated in the book *Do What You Love, The Money Will Follow,* by Marsha Sinetar, Ph.D. I've heard so many people espouse this thought, and I've read so many books based on it, that for a long time I assumed it must be true.

It's a seductive idea. Who wouldn't like to believe that, by thinking good thoughts and doing what we love, we'll be opening doors through which wealth will find its way into our lives? In fact, it was through this particular lens that I'd listened to what Richard had said. And yet, it didn't match my experience. No matter how much I love running, for example, my penguin legs will never carry me to fame and fortune. And after twenty-five years of competitive running and swimming, I think it's safe to say that I've given the theory a fair test. Consequently, I think the title should be changed to *Do What You Love, Satisfaction Will Follow*. This much, anyone can prove for himself.

I realized that what Richard meant is that identifying with our own thoughts increases our defensiveness. When I asked him, "Why should I straighten the house, when I'm paying somebody else to do it?" I was defending my own position, and in the process I was hurting myself and my relationship with Chris. This is the lesson we are supposed to learn when the Course in Miracles instructs us to ask ourselves *Would you rather be right or would you rather be happy?*

Maybe in the end our thoughts do create our reality, but not necessarily in the way we want or expect them to. Maybe it isn't all the big muscular affirmations we repeat to ourselves every day in an attempt to control our destiny ("I am abundant in love and money"), but rather all the little unseen identifications with our thoughts ("I hate paying tolls") that shape our outlook without our even knowing.

It would be a long time before I would come to this understanding. In the meantime, I was still wearing a pair of glasses that I'd forgotten I put on.

4

Running With Marc

"In the middle of the road of my life
I awoke in a dark wood
Where the true way was wholly lost."
   —Dante

Just *try* thinking your way out of a depression!"

I was stunned. I'd never heard Marc's voice so clipped and humorless. We were running an out-and-back course we called the Brickyard after an old brick factory at the turn-around. Pushing my son Zach in his Baby Jogger II, I struggled to keep up. The trail veered in and out along the cliffs that overlook Carquinez Strait, at the extreme northeast corner of San Francisco Bay. The challenging course rises and plunges over fingers of land extending out into the Bay. Four tough hills on the way out, the same four hills on the return.

I hadn't seen Marc in a while. I'd just finished telling him about the conversation with Richard while we floated on the waves, and I'd advanced the notion that our thoughts create our reality. Clearly I'd struck a nerve.

"I just came through a bout of depression, and it scared me," Marc said. "It's been twenty years and more since I felt like that. I went to a counselor, and she was very helpful."

The thought of a depressed Marc was too much. He's always been the lighthouse for others in their personal darkness. "Running with you is so uplifting, it's hard to imagine you ever being depressed. Are you okay now? Why didn't I find out about this earlier?"

"I'm fine," he said. "I have an idea about it—it's not my idea, it's Larkin's, and I think he's right."

I don't know Larkin very well. Another club runner, he'd experienced a great deal in his life. A physician, a deep thinker, and a loner, I knew he'd conquered bouts of depression and substance abuse, and that he'd been divorced as a consequence.

Marc continued, "Larkin told me, 'Mood underlies everything.' He believes all the self-help positive thinkers have it backward, that it isn't our thoughts that dictate our moods, but our moods that create our thoughts. To use your analogy: Mood is the ocean, and thoughts are the waves. Depending on your mood, you may have very different thoughts about the same circumstances."

We crested the fifth hill and I lengthened my stride, allowing the weight of Zach's stroller to pull me along. I took deep breaths to regroup for the next ascent. From somewhere below, a barking seal caught Zach's attention. "Doggie!" he cried.

"It sounds like a doggie, Zach. That's a seal. He lives in the ocean."

"Oseen," Zach said, extending an index finger to the blue. I thought about moods as my eyes lingered on the big bulge of water that Zach had pointed to. Such unimaginable depths.

"That's right, little man." I said. The alpenglow of sunset illuminated the top of Zach's head, the pink light exaggerating the angry red of his eczema. Zach smiled and leaned forward, touching the turning wheels of his oversized stroller as we rolled downhill.

"Did the counselor help?" I asked.

"She was very good. When you've been married for as long as I have, you notice the repeating patterns. There are arguments the Frog and I have rehashed for thirty years. It finally got to me, and the counselor helped."

"The Frog" is Marc's beautiful French-descended wife. Sweethearts since high school, Jenny and Marc are mutual counterpoints, balancing each other out. Marc will think nothing of investing ten thousand dollars based on a radio report about a new product, while Jenny will consult four investment newsletters and calculate the beta before jumping in. Jenny has watched Marc segue from alcoholism to sobriety, from high-powered executive at Exxon to self-employed Closet Magican, from chain smoker to Hawaiian Ironman triathlete. She's the rock Marc needed to set his moorings, the Yin to his Yang. Together, they've raised a son, Dave, of whom they are both proud, though Jenny worries that Marc's jaundiced views on corporate hierarchy will forever taint Dave's ability to work within the mainstream.

Marc and Jenny share much common experience and mutual admiration. Marc has put Jenny on a pedestal, for having endured his stumbles and missteps. Jenny, who's seen it all, smiles at the people who gravitate to her husband in his role as the running club's elder statesman and prophet-of-meaning.

I felt stunned by Marc's revelation. To hear about his depression and realize that he and Jenny had fought was almost too much to absorb. I wobbled in my stride, distracted, and Zach giggled at the sudden side-to-side motion. Marc and I had run together nearly a hundred times, and in all those runs, aside from rare bursts of vapid male humor, Marc had said nothing disparaging about Jenny. Perhaps naively, I'd carried an image of their relationship, a comfortable certainty that after years of marriage, some couples come to a loving understanding, having transcended the bickering that plagues newer relationships. In my mind, Marc and Jenny had graduated.

I'd come to this belief despite fifteen years of my own very good marriage, in which I'd learned that all marriages, even the good ones, demand vigilance. Growth means change. Change causes friction. Jenny and Marc had lived through their share of change. In an odd way, that thought cheered me, because it could mean that the pettinesses that crept into my own marriage weren't terminal. I wanted to know more. I, too, had experienced cyclic disagreements of marriage, and I wanted to find out how to break the cycle.

I said, "How did the counselor help?"

"She reminded me that it takes two people to play tennis. When you're in a match that you don't want to be in, stop playing. Just set the racquet down."

We'd reached the bottom of the next-to-last hill. Zach began to squirm. "Baba," he said, demanding his bottle. I stopped and pulled out the Isomil soy formula.

"Here you go, buddy bear," I said. Zach let out a tiny whine of pleasure, his right hand grabbing the bottle as his left reached for his head. He drank and scratched, settling in his seat. We'd been running for nearly an hour, and it was getting late. Zach was tired. I resumed pushing, leaning hard into the stroller on the climb. "What does that mean, 'set your racquet down'?"

"Like I said, mood underlies everything. For example, for years, the Frog and I have had differences about my people and her people. Most of the time, it's not an issue, but if one of us is in a bad mood, we always seem to talk about it, speaking our minds in an attempt to 'work on our communication.' The funny thing is, when we're in a good mood, our families are seldom an issue. The only thing that changes is the mood. Viewing the same situation in a good mood, I can find nothing to confront her about."

We crested the hill and began the last descent. Again, Zach's weight pulled me along. I reached down and stroked his head. "Okay, I see the pattern. I've seen it a thousand times. But what does it mean to put your racquet down?"

"It always comes down to self-awareness, recognizing the mood you're in. When you learn to recognize your moods, you begin to respect the power of a low mood to paint everything in dark, problematic hues. The great seduction is the thought that you can solve your problems at that time. Learn to keep your mouth shut till you're feeling better. Then decide if it's still an issue. The best way not to play tennis is not to show up. If you can have the self-awareness to recognize the mood and the discipline to shut up, you'll suffer far fewer confrontations. And the funny thing is, the bad mood will pass quicker, and you'll learn to discount what other people say when they're in a bad mood."

Marc had said something big. I knew I'd need to live with it for a while. For now, I needed a diversion. "Are you suggesting we should try to manage our own moods? Do you support the use of antidepressants?" I said, aware of the controversy surrounding Prozac.

"Prescribed by a doctor, I'm all for them. Larkin says they help a lot of patients who would be lost without them. What do you think?"

I smiled. I'd set Marc up, and it had worked. "I'm strongly pro-Zach, but then I'm his dad, and to me his diaper doesn't stink."

"Not bad." Marc laughed.

We reached the bottom of the hill, and Zach tossed his empty bottle out the side of the Baby Jogger. I stopped to pick it up. Bits of gravel stuck to the moist nipple, and I shoved it into a side pocket. Zach let out a cry, scratching the top of his head with both hands, his face contorted in a familiar frozen wince. I flinched inwardly, unable to do anything to make him comfortable. "Here, Zach, play with the turtle," I said weakly, handing him a plastic toy. "We'll go home soon."

"Poor little guy," Marc said. "He really looks uncomfortable. These allergies are serious, aren't they?"

"Life-threatening," I said. "A glass of milk could literally kill him." My mood rose or fell along with my hopes for helping Zach's allergies. Now, it was low.

Marc said, "With all the crap they put in milk today—the bovine growth hormone and so on—he's probably better off."

"I saw an *X Files* episode about what they put in milk. I'm sure it's an alien conspiracy," I joked.

Marc continued, "I met a lady in Georgia, a 102-year-old doctor who still practices medicine. She doesn't work long hours, but she sees patients every day. I asked her what her secret was, and do you know what she said? She said she never eats dairy products."

I smiled. Marc was on a roll. Even Zach had stopped scratching and was staring at Marc as he rattled on about hormones in milk that caused girls to menstruate prematurely. We reached the top of the final hill and passed through the old Martinez cemetery. Our serious talk about depression and Zach's health had segued into optimistic chatter about the benefits of Zach's restricted diet. "Children who drink milk have a higher incidence of attention deficit disorder and autism,"[1] Marc said. It was all downhill to the car.

As I loaded Zach in the car, I tried to sort out whether moods create thoughts, or thoughts create moods. I tended to throw in my lot with the pick-yourself-up-by-the-bootstraps crowd. Surely positive thinking creates a positive mood. Riffling through the archives of experience, though, I realized that I actually knew just two things. First, it's a lot easier to think positive thoughts when I'm in a good mood. Second, a run, whether good or bad, almost always elevates my mood. When it comes to creating good moods, endorphins trump

[1] As usual, Marc was on a roll that day. He often says things for effect—this time to cheer me up. This claim has been made about milk, but it is considered controversial.

positive thoughts every time.

Zach had fallen asleep in the back seat. His temporary relief from the itching gladdened me. On the drive home, I recalled a story I'd heard twenty years earlier, about a wise Chinese farmer.

> One day, a wise farmer's best horse ran away. The farmer's neighbor said, "Your best horse ran away. You won't be able to harvest your crops. What bad luck!"
>
> The wise farmer said, "Good luck, bad luck, who can say?" The next day, the farmer's horse returned, bringing with it thirty wild stallions and immediately transforming the farmer into a wealthy man.
>
> The farmer's neighbor said, "Thirty wild stallions! What good luck you have!"
>
> The wise farmer replied, "Good luck, bad luck, who can say?" The next day, the farmer's son was training the most beautiful of the wild stallions when he fell off the horse, breaking his leg.
>
> The farmer's neighbor said, "Your son has broken his leg. Now you have no one to help you harvest your crops. What bad luck you have!"
>
> The wise farmer said, "Good luck, bad luck, who can say?" The next day, the military came and conscripted all of the town's able-bodied young men to fight in the war.

I like the story for the many subtle lessons it veils. In a way, Marc had just retold it. As Zach's parent, I would gladly take on his eczema in order to free him from the terrible itching. I can't see Zach's discomfort as anything but painful, thus I can only judge it as bad. I feel I must do everything in my power to relieve his misery. I can't see how, in a possible interpretation of the story of the Chinese farmer, admonishments to suspend judgment would ever hold much weight with me.

When we encounter real suffering, we must try to relieve it. Any parent would agree. Only an intellectualizing non-parent would argue differently. In fact, when the farmer's son broke his leg, it's only natural to assume that he helped cast his son's leg. He surely didn't sit around saying, "Good luck, bad luck, who can say?"

Another side of Zach's situation ties it to the wise farmer. In fact, Marc had just reminded me of it.

In the past, I had held needless collateral judgments around Zach's condition. I'd lamented missing a job opportunity in Tokyo because we couldn't read food labels in Japanese, and because Zach's medications weren't available in Japan. But I don't actually know if working in Japan would have turned out to be a good experience.

Chris and I disliked the vacation restrictions that Zach's food preparation placed us under, limiting us in where we could go and the lodgings where we could stay. But how could we feel bad about vacations that we hadn't planned or taken? I had worried that Zach's inability to share a pizza would isolate him when he reached high school age. The truth is, I don't know what the future holds. Perhaps medicine will advance to the point where Zach's diet will no longer be an issue. Maybe someday Zach won't be able to go into a pizza parlor, and there'll be a drive-by shooting, and his life will be spared. Who can say? If I'm honest, I can't.

It doesn't help to get worked up over things that haven't happened yet, in any case, or things that are outside our control. Everyone knows this; the real question is how you stop getting worked up. How do you stop judging events as "good" or "bad"? Telling ourselves not to worry makes us worry about worrying. A perfect psychological tail-chase. So how do we vanquish our imaginary worries? Marc gave me a clue. The secret, he said, lies in paying attention. Attention is the precursor to changing our moods and thoughts. It's the golden key.

5

Running With Big Jack

"The great soul is the person who has taken on the task of change. If he or she is able to transcend fear, to act out of courage, the whole of its group will benefit and each one, in his or her own life, will be suddenly more courageous, though they may not see how or why." —Gary Zukav, *Seat of the Soul*

When a cellular service company chooses an equipment supplier, it must live with the decision for at least a decade, thanks to what is called the "high barrier to exit." It costs a cellular service provider about a hundred million dollars to acquire the real estate and infrastructure for the first phone call in an average-sized city, and it costs thirty million dollars per year thereafter to provide service and expand network capacity. Thus, picking a manufacturer is a major decision, since replacing cellular infrastructure is even more difficult than building it. Aside from the huge expense involved, it can't be done without interrupting service and angering customers.

In the world of cellular, then, it was a very big deal when SkyReach decided to replace DeciBell cellular infrastructure with our company's RadioGear equipment in its flagship Los Angeles market in 1988. Now, nine years later, SkyReach had grown impatient with the poor reliability of RadioGear's network and software delivery schedules in the Los Angeles area. Amid this tumult, I opened a RadioGear office at SkyReach headquarters in Walnut Creek, California. I was responsible for overall sales and for RadioGear's relationship with this customer.

Every six months, I would arrange a day-and-a-half meeting between the senior management staffs of SkyReach Domestic Operations and RadioGear Cellular Infrastructure. The meeting format was a morning of shared visions and industry outlook, followed by an afternoon of golf and an evening of cocktails and dinner. But the real meeting began on the morning of the second day. That's when SkyReach usually aired its grievances, enumerating the losses it had incurred thanks to problems with RadioGear's equipment and deliveries. For those wearing RadioGear name tags, the recommended attire was a bulletproof Kevlar vest. Still, I looked forward to the meetings because they were always first-class events, and they allowed me to spend time with Big Jack, the president of our division within RadioGear.

We called him Big Jack because he managed a division of thirteen thousand people worldwide, representing four billion dollars in annual revenues, and the "Big Jack" moniker distinguished him from one of his lieutenants, who was known as "Little Jack." I believed, though, that he'd acquired the name because of his unmistakable personal force, energy, and presence. I once mentioned this to my boss, who laughed and said, "You'd have presence, if you made two million a year."

Before the semiannual executive summit meeting, Big Jack would call my office every day for a week to be briefed on the latest developments. During a typical week, we would receive calls from Tokyo the first day, Beijing the next, followed by Hong Kong, Singapore, and Sydney, culminating with Big Jack's arrival in California. During one daily briefing call, I was having trouble hearing him because of a shooshing noise in the background. "Jack, this is a terrible connection—I can hardly hear you. Where are you?"

"I've got you on the cell phone. I'm taking a shower."

To me, Big Jack is Hemingway in wingtips. He's brilliant, driven, works all hours, yet manages to run well enough to meet the qualifying time for the Boston Marathon. Oh, and he's a seven-handicap golfer, mountain climber, and connoisseur of fine wines. Though I wouldn't trade my experience for his, Big Jack is what Hemingway would have called a Man, written large.

The executive summit was being held at Carmel Valley Lodge, and on the morning of the second day I left my room at 5:30 A.M., in time for an hour's run and a quick shower before 7:00, when the the RadioGear negotiating team would meet to prepare for the session with SkyReach. The big issue this year was SkyReach's displeasure with our overall network performance in Los Angeles. SkyReach claimed that our failure to deliver features and functionality had cost them forty million dollars in lost market share and stock value. I agreed with their complaint, if not their numbers. My recommendation to Big Jack included a package of equipment and services worth approximately twenty-five million dollars. I hadn't chosen that number by accident—I'd borrowed it from other customer negotiations that Jack had participated in. Big Jack had responded from Singapore that he'd give ten million and no more, and he'd laid out alternative plans for earning an agreement.

I ran through the resort gardens, picking up the golf cart path along the fourteenth fairway, when Big Jack fell in stride with me. "Jack," I said, "I'm surprised to see you." Respect and amazement colored my voice. As a junior member at these affairs, my role included closing the evening with customers who might wish to stay up drinking and talking. The night before, Big Jack had lingered until the bitter end, at 12:30 A.M. I had followed my standard policy of taking no alcoholic beverages and listening as much as possible. Meanwhile, Big Jack had drunk enough Jordan Cabernet to bring down a bull elephant. I didn't expect to see him until the morning session; even then, I wondered how much of the proceedings I'd end up having to lead. Yet here he was, looking his usual energetic self. I'd never seen anything like it.

"Jack," I said after we'd run together for a few minutes, "why just ten million? Two weeks ago, you gave Mobile East Telephone thirty million for exactly the same shortfall, and they're not as big a customer as SkyReach."

Jack turned and smiled, morning fog and sweat glistening on his forehead. We left the pavement for a dirt trail that led up into the hills. Thick coastal vegetation lined the path, amply interlaced with poison oak. A young doe, startled, bounded into the woods. Jack then asked a question I would ask myself every time I entered a negotiation in subsequent years, because it encompassed everything I would ever need to know about a customer meeting.

"Dean, how's the relationship?"

"Well," I began, "it's terrible. Jack, it's worse than ever. They make no secret that they believe our failure to deliver has hurt their ability to compete. They think we intentionally make commitments we can't keep, to win business. They're openly hostile toward us. It's hard to get our people to come out and meet with them because it's so uncomfortable."

"And yet," Jack said, "according to J. D. Powers, they continue to be ranked number one in customer satisfaction, using our equipment?"

"Jack, they'll tell us they're number one *despite* our equipment. They say it's despite all the extra effort and expense they're forced to expend to get around the problems with our equipment. I don't think ten million will help matters. You and I both know they talk to Mobile East Telephone. SkyReach will find our offer insulting."

"Do you think giving them thirty million will make the situation any better?" Jack mused. "MET came to us with the same complaints as SkyReach. They laid out many of the same reasons they needed a certain feature, and how we had hurt them by not offering it yet. But MET limited their damages to legitimate ones, and they drew up a list of compromises they were willing to make to allow us to focus on the immediate problem. When we reallocate resources and slip on delivering something else, MET won't come back demanding payment for tardiness on those features, too. SkyReach will. MET understands that we depend on each other, and that we share common goals and purposes. MET works with us. SkyReach doesn't.

"We hurt SkyReach, and it's our job to make amends as best as we can, but our compensation should be appropriate to the damages and the situation. I find some of the items they're requesting remuneration for exaggerated and unethical. That's the real insult. We can't support this kind of cunning and deceit. It's not productive for either of us."

As the path grew steeper, my breathing quickened. We stopped talking. I dreaded the upcoming negotiations, knowing they would be heated and uncomfortable. Moisture dripped from the trees. As the slope grew more gentle, Jack turned and said, "So, how's Dean?"

"Getting a little worn down," I said. "I'm tired of getting beaten up in every meeting just because I wear a RadioGear badge. I'm losing my patience for it."

"Just remember," he said, "you're in purgatory with this account. You'll be delivered one day." As he finished speaking, we broke through the fog. Behind us, white fluffy clouds blanketed the coast, extending as far out over the Pacific as we could see. On the western horizon, a half-moon hung over the soft white canopy. The bright sunshine accentuated the brilliance of the scene. Above us, an emerald green peak rose two hundred feet against the backdrop of a cerulean blue sky. Jack and I continued upward. At the top of the hill, we stood absorbing the view and catching our breath.

Jack continued. "One of the things you have to remember is that RadioGear was, and will be, a great company. In the history of the cellular business, one company has always leap-frogged the rest. It'll be RadioGear's turn to make the jump again soon. A few short years ago, RadioGear and SkyReach together accomplished the equivalent of the first moon shot, by being the first in the world to launch digital cellular service. And we did it in the biggest city in the country. We've stumbled, but we will catch up again. The trouble is, SkyReach isn't the company you want to be stuck in a foxhole with."

I knew exactly what he meant. Big Jack often used military metaphors. He loved to tell a story from the Civil War, about a group of soldiers who were told to capture a bridge. Once the soldiers had taken the bridge, they sat down and drank coffee while the war continued to rage around them. Had the soldiers kept fighting, they'd have flanked the enemy, and their side would have won the battle. Instead, they lost. I think the story appealed to Big Jack because of his intense interest in being a leader and developing leaders. Big Jack wanted independent actors who could work within the larger picture of RadioGear. He wanted his people to take the bridge and flank the enemy. He backed up his belief in individual initiative by taking the time to teach his people to fight and win. It's the only reason I can think of that explains the events of the remainder of the day.

Responding to his foxhole comment, I said, "Yeah, and in the meantime we're gonna get fragged." We turned and started back down.

"No," he said. "You're looking at it all wrong. These negotiations are an unparalleled opportunity. This is where all the big forces of modern living come together for a few hours. Short of a life-and-death situation, nothing will ever be more intense. Millions of dollars will be on the table. Careers will be rising and falling. There will be politics within and between two organizations, and there will be as many personal agendas as there'll be people in the room. This is the ultimate crucible that our modern world can offer. This is where you'll find out what people are really like. Nobody can hide in a situation like this. Some will lose their temper. Some won't be able to act ethically when there are questions involving money. Some will cower in the background. Others will try to prove themselves by acting tough. This is where a person's true nature comes out. More importantly, this is where *your* true nature comes out. This is where you can see yourself, and meet your personal demons in the midst of all these powerful forces. The conditions will never be better." Jack grew silent as we descended into the fog.

My attention electrified by Jack's words, I said, "Can you elaborate on that?"

Jack said, "Four times in the past, we've negotiated agreements together. I've seen you in action. You're naturally gifted. You listen well. Against long odds, you try to find fair, reasonable solutions. I've also seen you walk away from a thirty-million-dollar contract when you thought the terms were too onerous, even though you would have benefited personally. That's why I trust you to do these things. There's really only one condition under which I've seen you lose your cool." I could feel Jack's silence, like a weight.

"What's that?" I said, not surprised to learn that Jack had seen me lose my cool. Often in these negotiations, I'd had to fight hard to contain my anger. But I was surprised that Jack had identified a single condition that set me off.

"That's something you're going to have to see for yourself. But I'll give you a hint. Observe yourself in today's session. Watch everything. Your body language. Your tone of voice. Everything. But most especially, just before you speak, *pay attention to your intentions for doing so*. If you can do that, you'll come to meet yourself, and it will transform you."

Jack declined to explain further. "See for yourself," he said, when I probed. We finished the run reviewing the complaints SkyReach would raise, and the right way to try to make them whole again. I reached my room at precisely 6:30.

The negotiations proceeded as if by a pre-authored script. SkyReach raised all the expected issues, giving all of the arguments about which I'd briefed our team. Big Jack handled the session with amazing skill, laying out the remuneration plan that he'd described to me, and bringing the package slowly down to ten million dollars. As is generally the case when senior executives meet, the negotiations were conducted on a more professional level than when people sitting on lower rungs of the organizational ladder attempt to resolve similar issues. In general, the meeting went much better than I had expected, at least until the end, when SkyReach surprised us with vigorous complaints regarding a particular machine in their network.

The machine was the first of its type in commercial service, and in the five years since the first unit had been installed, eight more had been supplied in Los Angeles. The replacement cost of each machine was approximately five million dollars. The machine in question had gone out of service several times in the last year, causing outages in parts of the digital network for reasons that could be traced back to both companies. SkyReach had failed to perform normal maintenance and upgrades. RadioGear had furnished faulty equipment. As often happens, the ultimate cause of the trouble wasn't clear; the machine was simply jinxed, and SkyReach demanded compensation for the troubles it had caused. From Radio-Gear's perspective, the machine had caused an inordinate amount of customer dissatisfaction.

Big Jack looked at me and said, "Dean, what do you think we ought to do?"

I said, "I think we should take a break and discuss this as a team."

Big Jack smiled and said, "No, I'm prepared to support your recommendation. Why don't you make a proposal to SkyReach."

Confusion spread like a mist, while a thousand thoughts raced in my head. *Big Jack had negotiated down to his ten-million-dollar limit. I had a career to consider. What was Big Jack thinking? What was he looking for? It was irresponsible to make a hard proposal before we'd met privately.* A familiar phrase came to mind, one that Big Jack had voiced often: *Do what's right for the customer and the relationship.* I knew what I would say.

"There's been a lot of finger-pointing in the past about this machine," I said, "Both sides have legitimate arguments. What I propose is that if RadioGear agrees to replace the machine at no charge to SkyReach, SkyReach will agree to pay for an audit of the other eight in the network, and to follow the upgrade recommendations proposed in the audit."

The offer felt right. In the short term, SkyReach would gain far more financially than RadioGear, but overall customer satisfaction would be put back on the right track. The offer took care of a disproportionate source of dissatisfaction, and helped ensure better network performance in the future. Glancing at Big Jack and my immediate boss, I could see that they were pleased.

The SkyReach team whispered among themselves as I sat and waited quietly, watching the animated discussion. Finally, the junior SkyReach employee, Tim, broke ranks and yelled, red-faced: "We accept your offer to replace the machine, but we don't accept the rest! Why should SkyReach have to pay for audits, which only tell us which of your faulty equipment we have to replace? You'll just tell us we have to buy more equipment to make up for the cost of the replacement, anyway. You should pay for the audits and the other upgrades, too."

Again, a thousand thoughts raced through my head. *What's so hard about understanding that you've got to maintain and upgrade equipment over time? I'll bet Tim has replaced the PC on his desk three times in the past five years. Why do these people always assume we're out to get them? Why does Tim always find a dark cloud in the silver lining? I stick my neck out with an offer to give them five million, and they come back with a response like that. It's unethical.* As I opened my mouth to respond, Jack's words from the morning's run came back to me: *Before you speak, pay attention to your intentions.* I froze.

I looked at my hands, which had been resting comfortably on my lap, and saw that my fingers were curled into fists, my wrists cocked tight. My shoulders, relaxed earlier, were hunched up to my neck and shoved forward. I thought: *What does this remind me of?* And I knew—I was a wild dog, angrily hunched over scraps of food. *But what's the food I'm hunched over?* As soon as I asked, the answer appeared before me: *Lack of recognition.* It wasn't money, career, or ethics that had so upset me. It was recognition. I was personally motivated by the impulse to treat others fairly, and in return I wanted to be recognized as generous and fair-minded. I wanted the moral high ground. Instead, I had received only a push-back, and my bruised ego wanted to fight. I realized that I was on the point of polluting the well of good intentions with the toxic refuse of my own, personal anger. My strength had turned to weakness. But I realized that there was more.

I distrust SkyReach's intentions in exactly the same way I just accused them of distrusting ours. All the bad feelings I carry from past negotiations are coloring my assessment of what's happening right now.

I laughed inwardly. It was all so clear. Tim and I shared a long history of similar negotiations. In calmer moments, we had talked informally and learned that we both felt good about parts of the meetings, and bad about others. Objectively, that meant we probably shared a good deal of common ground, affording our organizations a potential zone of agreement. But I knew also that Tim was deeply hurt by RadioGear's failure to meet some of its commitments, when he had stuck his neck out to recommend RadioGear as his company's supplier.

Tim had just reacted automatically, sucked in by the same blind impulse that I had nearly followed. It was a tiny acorn of an impulse, celebrated often in our society as the honest reaction of a "tough negotiator" and a "good businessperson." But those were only names for outward behaviors. Underneath, I could see the acorn for what it was: the seed of conflict. With a little water and coaxing, the acorn would swiftly grow into the oak of battle that had cast its shadow over the Bosnians and Serbs, the Protestants and Catholics. If SkyReach and RadioGear were ever going to improve their relationship, peace had to begin now, here in my own heart, before any words came out. I knew what I had to do. Having observed my own intentions, I spoke.

My anger replaced with the wonder of fresh insight, speaking in a calm, even, unemotional voice that I scarcely recognized, I said, "I put forth a proposal that I believed acknowledges the responsibility we share to serve your customers. I thought it was both fair and forward-looking. I'm open to suggestions about how we can improve it, but I'm not convinced that RadioGear should have to pay for everything." There were the words, most likely the same ones I'd have used even if I hadn't checked my intentions, but the delivery was radically different. It carried no tone that said *How could you be so unethical and greedy as to ask for more?* And it deeply affected what happened next.

The room fell silent. Even now, I don't know why nobody spoke, even to whisper among themselves. No one moved or said anything, the silence stretching longer than most people are accustomed to in our culture. In such quiet, the impulse to say something, merely to break the silence, begins to pinball inside, gaining momentum from the speed bumpers of personal agendas, until the tension of impasse must be released, often with a concession. I'd observed a similar quiet on many occasions in tense negotiations, but this time I felt no discomfort. I wondered if the other members of my team did. If so, they resisted the urge to speak, recognizing that the ball was in SkyReach's court. Two full minutes later, the senior-ranking SkyReach person said, "Your proposal is fair. We accept." Negotiations had never played like this between our companies; usually there had been belligerence and brinkmanship, but not this time. For the moment, at least, we had peace.

Within a year, Big Jack left RadioGear to become CEO of a telecommunications start-up. Because of his name and reputation, the company launched a most successful IPO, as a consequence of which Big Jack is now worth several hundred million dollars. At RadioGear, it became fashionable to blame Big Jack for any subsequent problems with product quality and delivery. People argued that he'd promised too much to too many customers. I disagreed. Run-of-the-mill managers are driven by fear and suffer the attendant side effects in the form of extreme need for control and displays of admiration. Big Jack was that rare treasure in the corporate hierarchy, driven by higher purpose and committed to motivating others and creating leaders. Many recoiled from the challenge.

Big Jack hired other people to address operations while he worked the customer side. The lieutenants Big Jack selected made serious product choice blunders that caused RadioGear's cellular infrastructure to fall behind. Through the sheer force of his personal commitment and charisma, Big Jack had kept RadioGear in the game a bit longer than its time. Along the way, he'd given me possibly the most important advice I'd received: *Pay attention to your intentions.*

Looking back, I understood that in the moment when I paid attention during the negotiation, I won my first real taste of professional freedom. I'd begun the process of extracting my personal identity from the job.

6

Well, I'll Be
a Runner's Uncle

*"Consider all this, and then turn to this green, gentle and most
docile earth; consider then both the sea and the land and do you
not find a strange analogy to something in yourself? For as this
appalling ocean surrounds the verdant land, so in the soul of man
there lies one insular Tahiti, full of peace and joy, but encompassed by all the horrors of the half known life."*
—Herman Melville, *Moby-Dick*

Backpacking is the wise, experienced uncle of running.
After graduating from UCLA, I spent the summer of 1982
backpacking from California to Alaska with my brother Mike
and a friend, Bob. I carried no camera, a decision I've sometimes regretted, and I wore no watch, which I've never regretted. I recently found my journal from the trip, and as I reread
it I saw kernels of nearly every thought and feeling that has
germinated in my life since that time. Reflecting on what I'd
written, I realized that running is my personal bridge

between the minimalist spiritual life of Thoreau and the life I'm leading as family man and corporate executive in the modern material world.

"Stuff is like an anchor," I wrote in that summer's journal. What I meant by "stuff" is the accumulation of possessions that can hold a person rooted psychically and physically in one place. One of the many beauties of backpacking is that it brings the true nature of possessions into high relief. Whatever you bring, you'll have to carry it, step by step, mile after mile, forging streams and cresting mountain passes. When you backpack, luxury must be weighed (literally!) against burden.

The modern world makes it all too easy for us to overlook the burden of possessions. We've all known people who worked at jobs they barely tolerated, solely to afford a luxurious home, then sought a promotion so they could buy an expensive car that they thought would make the commute more bearable. And so on and on, in an infinite series of cause–effect loops from which nobody ever seems to break free.

We Americans no longer seem to even notice the psychic burdens that attach to the possessions we so ardently desire. We invite these comforts and conveniences into our lives as guests, and they become our masters. A backpacker feels this directly. The sport translates the psychic burdens of possession into palpable, physical ones. A backpacker knows that creature comforts come at a price he literally can't carry, so he doesn't invite much luxury to join him on the trail.

With few possessions to worry him, the backpacker becomes an ascetic in pursuit of transmaterial quarry, a particular variety of spiritual experience. That experience is hard to attain when we're spinning in relentless cycles of desire for material goods. To make room for this spiritual experience, the backpacker attends to material matters with great thoughtfulness and care. Food must be sufficiently nourishing to support the effort of hiking long distances, but not so heavy that it weighs the journey down. Other items must support basic survival needs, and with a little ingenuity, they may serve multiple functions. If we attended to our everyday lives with similar care, we would avoid many self-inflicted troubles.

"Why am I anesthetized from my own life?" I wrote in my journal on June 27, 1982. I also wrote: "Why do I choose the television set when I could be out here instead? Sleeping on the ground keeps me close to the Earth, slowing my three-minute-now-a-word-from-our-sponsor mind down, allowing me to hear the longer, deeper rhythms around me."

I had already begun to explore the notion that our culture is based on managing pain and discomfort. If we're bored— well, we mustn't *allow* ourselves to be bored. We'll turn on the television set or raid the refrigerator. If we're stressed, we can turn to alcohol. Feeling run down or in a low mood? We can turn to caffeine. (I write these words with a cup of coffee cradled in my lap.) All in the name of avoiding discomfort.

I'm anesthetized when I try to hold the unpleasantnesses of my own life at arm's length, not realizing that it's these dark moments that leaven the bread of compassion. Without that very basic food, we're left hungry, estranged, and disconnected from the human experience of our lives, too weak to nurture others in their dark times.

I sometimes think that fifty percent of real spirituality is ordinary self-acceptance. I love the moment when two people interact, and one has the courage to admit to an unflattering emotion, and the other has the confidence and self-awareness to admit to having experienced the same ugly feeling. The other day, I was talking to another parent as he pushed his son on the swing a the park. He was waxing poetic about how much he liked being a dad, and how the experience fulfilled him. I looked at him and said, "I love most of it, but I have to admit that when I'm trying to put a diaper on Zach and he gets up and runs away, I don't always feel so joyful and fulfilled."

The other father laughed and agreed readily. In that moment of honesty, we moved closer to the kind of self-acceptance that will be needed in our culture if we're ever to bridge the systemic isolation that plagues us. Usually, it's the very things we hide about ourselves that we dislike in others. When we stop hiding, we can enjoy life more fully. When I don't have a personal agenda, it's funny sometimes when

Zach scampers away naked during a diaper change. Years ago, as a young backpacker, I wrote about feeling "anesthetized" from my life. At the time, I couldn't foresee the frustrations of a kid running naked down the hall. But I did see, at least abstractly, that hiding from frustrations causes problems.

When I wrote about my fears of living a "now-a-word-from-our-sponsor" existence, I contrasted that life with the world of the backpacker, who consciously tries to remove the external distractions, interruptions, and advertisements of the modern world. Then, only the mind's own shameless tricks remain as a final barrier to direct experience.

Even the mind can't stand alone. In the wilderness, away from cultural influences, the backpacker can't avoid confronting the immensity of nature. The mountains sit like giant Buddhas, the backpacker's all-day hike but a passing itch in the endless metabolism of Earth, the lifetime of a man but a single day. And compared to Earth itself, even the long, silent meditations of the great mountains are but a passing fortnight; the plate-tectonic collision of continents a fleeting adolescent angst. And compared to the stars, the life of Earth is but a year. And so it goes on.

The logical mind contemplating infinities is compelled to twist them into conclusions it can comprehend. "Life is meaningless," it decides. "The lives and works of the greatest among us crumble to dust, insignificant in the enormity of endless time. What's the point?" But even our feelings of futility, when faced with this enormity, aren't our most genuine experience. Feelings of meaninglessness are the constructs of an everyday mind attempting to cope and weakly tempting us to succumb. But there's something else, behind our dark suspicions of meaninglessness. Our most genuine experiences in nature occur outside the grasp of the logical mind, out of reach of language. The deeper, more authentic experience is a sensation of great peace, a profound feeling of belonging, an unfathomable knowing that everything is exactly as it should be, and that our lives have meaning. This is the experience that backpackers seek.

Against the backdrop of the infinite side of nature, we see that we are but a gentle gathering and receding of the universe. We begin as the union of two cells, and we finish as plant food. Between, there is only the experience of our lives. This experience, the good and the bad, the transcendent and the mundane, is the only real wealth we can ever have. We are a one-time-only, unique expression of the cosmos. Viewed in this context, we know the importance of finding and fulfilling our purpose in life. It's only when we lose touch with what I called "the long rhythms" in my journal that we lose the sense of peace and belonging that come from listening to those long rhythms. Cut off from this deeper music, we find life terrifying. Then the ego steps in to try to manage the terror.

In 1982, I wrote: "I would do well to keep my possessions down to an amount that can be carried in a single carload." Unfortunately, I didn't have the courage to follow my own advice. I was in a hurry to build a future, and I pushed aside my yearnings for self-discovery and spiritual growth in favor of the conventional societal encouragements of the day. Instead of following the path of my own questions, I chose to pursue the more traditional path of a corporate career, with its myriad distractions from the inner search. I don't regret the experience. It may have been necessary for my spiritual development; now, at least I know the corporate world for what it is. My only regret is that I was willing to derail my search for inner meaning for fifteen years while I built a career. It would take Zach's birth to jolt me into taking up those questions again. Perhaps Zach would be able to live with more courage than his father, and shortcut those needless detours.

I know of a surefire, authentic spiritual experience that's available to nearly everyone, but it comes at a cost that I think most people are unwilling to pay. Take five days out of your life and head into the wilderness on foot, making sure to stay out of earshot of anything that translates the burning of fossil fuels into forward motion.[2] Even if you experience none of

---

[2] Alone or with friends. But before you set out for the wilderness with a sack of rice and a song, take the time to learn how to equip yourself, and learn the ground rules of backcountry etiquette.

the sublime joys and sense of belonging that I've attempted to portray—even if you just have a downright miserable time—you'll see the world in a new way when you emerge.

Viewed through eyes sharpened by deprivation, a grocery store looks like a flat-out miracle. The modern grocery gets my nomination as the twentieth century's defining achievement. It's Shangri-la, Sodom and Gomorrah, and the Seven Wonders of the World all in one, with its pyramids of shiny fruit and hanging gardens of leafy vegetables. And it's a Dante's Purgatory of excess with its 284—I've counted them—varieties of cookies. Do we *need* that many cookies? So long as there are Oreos, no, we don't. The neighborhood supermarket is a visible tribute to the vast networks of people and technology that bring all this food together, fit to eat. The fact that we can eat grapes year-round is a genuine wonder. And I think it's a damnation upon us every time we take it for granted.

How big a crisis is it, really, when the supermarket runs out of Frosted Mini Wheats? Most Americans wouldn't endure a week without the local market, and I'd be among the first to perish. Five days of deprivation would convince us that refrigeration is a luxury almost beyond imagining—a pleasure that's almost impossible to describe when indulged in the form of an ice-cold Coca-Cola after a week of sweating under a heavy backpack.

Common pleasures experienced after voluntarily depriving

ourselves are known as if for the first time. It's like landing on another planet; you'll never know Earth in quite the same way again. To appreciate how good things are at home, we must go into the wilderness.

7

Backpacking With Jared

"Climb the mountains and get their good tidings. Nature's peace will flow into you as sunshine flows into trees. The winds will blow their own freshness into you, and the storms their energy, while cares will drop off like autumn leaves."
—John Muir, *Our National Parks*

Going into the wilderness takes courage.

Nine months before Zach was born, I went backpacking in the Sierras with my young nephew, Jared. I was hoping that Jared would discover something of the inner experience of the wilderness for himself. If nothing else, I figured he might learn that his evening dose of SportsCenter wasn't essential for a fulfilling life.

Our first trip together went well, and four months after Zach was born, we set out on another. Jared was thirteen at the time, just about to enter high school, and I was mindful to gear the trip to his abilities. We'd hike five and a half miles in on the first day, spend the next day fishing and climbing, hike back out again on the third day, celebrating with a hot shower and Skurfburger at Ducey's Bass Lake Lodge.

Whenever I'd spent time with Jared before, it had generally taken him a day or so to begin to open up. On this trip, I could tell that there was something weighing on his mind, and I wondered if he had a new girlfriend. I knew that if I waited, Jared would talk. On the second day, we climbed 10,400-foot Mount Madera—Jared's first summit. At the end of the day, after we'd cooked dinner and washed the dishes and hung our food in a tree, out of the reach of bears, I sensed that Jared was exhausted but elated. "Uncle Dean," he asked, "how important are grades?"

So that's what's eating him, I thought. The question didn't surprise me. Just before we left, my sister-in-law Mardi told me that Jared had been slacking off in school. Mardi felt that Jared was back on track. She'd read that at some point in their teens, most boys stop trying in school, and that the earlier the problem occurs, the more easily it can be corrected. Even though I knew about the problem, I gave Jared an answer that fell short of the advice he really needed. I told him that he was now at the age when colleges would examine his transcripts and to get into a good school, he would have to earn good grades.

Jared is the overachiever type of kid who seldom questions the common social wisdom. Driven to excel in sports and school, he didn't seem likely to question the importance of grades. I worried that I'd missed an important opportunity. If Zach ever asked the same question, I didn't want to fall short. That night, sitting by the flickering fire and watching the Big Dipper perform its long, slow stir around the North Star, I wrote a letter to Zach, in the notebook where I'd kept my journal in the summer of 1982:

Dear Zach,

I have taken your cousin Jared out for our second annual backpacking trip together. I look forward to sharing this experience with you too. I hope that when you are old enough, I am still able, because there is something out here that I want you to experience. Tonight, Jared asked me a question that I remember asking my dad, so I think it safe to assume you will ask it someday too. He asked: "Uncle Dean, are grades important?"

I smiled, reminiscing for a brief moment, and gave to Jared the same answer my father gave to me a quarter century ago. I explained that yes, grades are important. I told Jared that he is about to enter high school and that colleges look at grades as a measure of the quality of the applicant. And in today's information age, a college degree is the minimum price of admission for good-paying jobs. To have any real choice about how to make a living in our society, you need to do your schoolwork.

I felt a little uncomfortable with the answer I gave Jared, because it was far from the whole story. When you were born, I promised myself I would be as truthful as I could be about what I had learned in my life, in the hope that you might avoid some of the detours I took. And so now, here is the rest of the story as I see it. This idea that "right" grades are important to get into the "right" college can be but the first link in a whole chain of social attitudes. The chain continues something like this: Once you get into the "right" college, you still must earn good grades to get the "right" job. Once you get the "right" job, you must work hard to earn a "right" review so you can get a promotion to the next "right" job. And so on.

What remains unsaid is that behind each link in this chain lies a certain fear: the fear of failure in the eyes of others, and the attending notion that others know better about what is good for you than you do. What people don't recognize is that when they pick up the first link of this conventional wisdom chain— "getting good grades is important"—they usually adopt the conventional fears behind it, too. Worse yet, by picking up the first link, they pick up the whole necklace, and unwittingly adopt a way of life. It is an easy trap to fall into, and it never ends. The necklace might as well be a noose. Don't get me wrong, Zach. Good grades and a good career are not evil or sinful or wrong pursuits in and of themselves. The only problem with getting good grades or having a good career is that people who have them tend to identify with good grades and a good career, becoming too absorbed in them, losing the notion that they themselves in essence are not those things. But this does not mean you should stop striving for good grades. I hope that my own experience will demonstrate why I think this way.

Now, I have something to confess. I did not understand exactly what it was I was taking on when

I was Jared's age and decided grades were important. So sometimes I cheated in high school. I didn't cheat on everything or even all that often, because I had "standards." I never cheated in math or science, the courses I considered to be "real," because the knowledge was derivative and I knew the importance of understanding lines of reasoning. The lone exception to this rule was complex formula memorization—because I rationalized that in real life I could always look them up in a book anyway. The softer classes such as history, social studies and the like I played by ear. If I considered the information to be banal, I cheated if I had to. The same was true if I felt the task was an exercise in rote memory, such as learning dates. Finally, one day, I got caught copying off somebody else's paper. Although I didn't recognize it at the time, the fear I inherited with the desire to get good grades bubbled right to the surface—just like a knee-reflex response to a doctor's hammer. *What is going to happen to my transcripts?* I wondered. The only punishment I received were these words that everybody hears, but nobody understands—not even the people saying them: When you cheat, you are only hurting yourself. *Yeah right,* I thought at the time, *I'm hurting myself right into a good college.*

What I didn't understand in high school was that I really was only hurting myself. Each time I cheated, I chose personal gain over facing the consequences of my actions. But this gain came at a price I did not recognize at the time: the erosion of my own personal courage. Now, before I can go on, Zach, you must understand two things. First, the only way to have a meaningful life is to follow your own, authentic path. You cannot deceive yourself about whether or not you are on your own path, because part of you will always know if it is true or not. And, second, choosing your own path in life requires real courage. You cannot look to somebody else's paper for direction. And yet, even today, this is always my first inclination. If I have a problem, I look for a book to supply me with an answer. Life doesn't work that way. Personal courage pools within us from many sources. One wellspring of courage comes from making legitimate efforts—in this case, doing the studies to earn good grades. Accumulation of hard-won courage takes time. We cannot afford to spill even one drop of it over a trivial matter such as grades we did not earn.

By the time I reached college, I had begun to recognize both the damage I was doing by cheating, and the fears I had adopted behind the grades. I rebelled by not studying. I always consoled myself about my performance, thinking *I could have done better if I had just studied*. This approach, too, proved wrong. Just because I turned my back on my fear, refusing to address it head-on, does not mean it went away. On the contrary, it multiplied, because I had now adopted the doubt of not really knowing what I could achieve. Fears are like that—you cannot ignore them. As much as we would like it to be otherwise, the only approach to dark fears is to expose them to the light of our attention—but this requires courage. So where, you might ask, does that leave us? Grades are important. Grades can come with fears. Not worrying about grades can intensify those fears. What is a young man to do?

It is not the usual case that high school or young college students know what they want to do with their lives. They may think that they do, but they really have no idea how much they will grow and change through their adult years. (By the way, Zach, growth is also the reason I advise against teenage tattoos and body piercing—I guarantee your taste in "art" will change.) Earning good grades keeps more doors of opportunity open. The only legitimate path that I can see for a student to take is to become a person without an alibi. Work hard, study, and show up without any excuses to fall back on. Then let the chips fall where they may. Try not to become too attached to the outcome of good grades themselves. Understand that you have done everything possible to influence the receipt of them, but you cannot control the final result. Life is like that—despite what the positive-thinking types say to the contrary, you cannot control outcomes. This approach of not becoming too attached to outcomes also becomes a spring source of courage. You will learn that outcomes don't matter nearly as much as we think they do. No matter what grades you receive, you will know that you have stood on your own and faced student life with courage. This courage will serve you well when it comes time to choose the path dictated by your own personal experience over the one the conventional wisdom tells us we should follow.

I wish for you all of the best in your own search for understanding and meaning.

Love,
Dad

8

Running With Marc

"All man's miseries derive from not being able to sit quietly in a room alone." —Blaise Pascal

A couple of months after the backpacking trip with Jared, Marc and I were running the up-and-down contours of a ridgeline overlooking the green valley that we both call home. As we ran, Marc said, "Young guys like you have it all over guys like me."

"What do you mean?" I asked.

"I look at you, and I can see that you already know what's important. As far as I can tell, you're happily married. You love your kid. You don't need extravagances. You haven't complicated your life with booze and womanizing. You haven't been sucked in by the idea that you need a bigger house or a better car. Of course, the corporate types are always a little suspicious of that. They know you won't sell your soul for a five-thousand-dollar-a-year raise. It's not that important to you."

"Marc, I think a lot of people know these things."

"Sure, some do. But it's not as common as you might think. Tell me, what's your idea of a perfect life? What would a perfect day look like?"

"That's easy," I said. "My perfect life would include waking up in the morning and going for a run. Then Chris and I would take Zach to school. I'd have a little one-room office above a store downtown with a view of the street, and I'd go there for five or six hours a day and read and write. In the middle, I'd take a break and hit the master's swim practice at Heather Farms."

"Yeah," Marc interrupted, "There's nothing like a noon workout when the sun's shining, and all the lanes are crowded with people who've made time in the middle of the day to swim. I love it! And I love shooting the breeze afterward. But I interrupted you. Go on."

"After the workout, I'd go back and write some more. When school let out, I'd meet Chris and we'd pick up Zach. In the evening, Zach would have a baseball game or a swim meet that we could attend. I might even coach his team."

Marc smiled. We were holding a steady, easy pace. "See what I mean? You know what's important. You aren't one of those guys who try to buy a new persona at The Gap. You already have most of the things you've just described."

"I don't think there are all that many people trying buy a new persona."

"You'd be surprised. Do you know how many times I've had guys tell me their perfect day would include eighteen holes at Pebble Beach, a roll in the hay with Cindy Crawford, a steak and a baked potato lathered in sour cream, and a cigar? They truly think that's what they want."

I said, "None of that sounds too terrible, especially the Cindy Crawford part."

"I agree, but my point is, it's a hollow vision of life. When you talked about your perfect day, you didn't include any big-ticket items. You don't need to be rich to live your perfect day."

"Having a lot of money would make it easier."

"That may be. But if I interpret what you said correctly, you don't really want the money. You want the freedom. Most guys think they need a lot of money, and they claim that working lots of hours stimulates and sustains them while they pursue the goal. But in the process they get lost. They think working and climbing is all there is to life. Without spending some time every day in contemplation, how can anybody claim to be nourishing their soul?"

I said, "That's right. I crave more solitude, too, and I think it's perhaps the most important thing a person needs. But having a little more money would help me buy that solitude.

However, I guess your point is that it's easy to get distracted by the big house, the fancy car, the trophy wife, and the image of success."

"That's what I'm saying. Look around. We have all of these time-saving devices, yet nobody ever has enough time. Dean, you hold down a big job, and you still manage to go for a run every day. You're able to find solitude in the midst of a demanding career and an active, committed family life. Why? Because you aren't distracted by the empty trappings. You know what's important. Are you aware just how long it took me to figure out what you already know?"

I enjoyed the praise, but I was also little embarrassed, and I steered the conversation in a new direction. For a while, we talked about cell phones, pagers, answering machines, TV, and the Internet, and how these technologies have impinged on every aspect of our lives, from dining out to pumping gas. Then Marc tossed off one of his trademark memorable sentences: "Yes, electronic demagogues rob us of the one thing we require to be truly free, our solitude."

Stunned, I stopped dead in my tracks. Now I understood why a run or a backpacking trip rejuvenates us.

I'd read an article in *Runners World* magazine that reported: "A Penn State University study found that after 20 minutes of aerobic exercise, a 'marked lessening' of left brain (analytical) activity occurs, which results in greater activity in the right (creative) hemisphere. But this shift occurs only if the exercise is relatively mindless and does not require continuous cognitive processing." My own experience definitely supported that finding. Answers to questions emerged, specific word phrasings blossomed, and all manner of new ideas flowed unobstructed as I ran, as if I were receiving a gift. When I ran, the quality of the experience was more creative and more enjoyable than the quality of ordinary thought. I had always wondered, if a person was truly more creative during a run, why hadn't natural selection chosen the running state of mind as our everyday condition? Why was running required to induce it? Marc's words filled the gap for me. Running gives us solitude.

It isn't that nature doesn't want us to be happy, creative thinkers. We simply allow ourselves to be distracted by unimportant things that block our creativity. When we backpack or run, we're alone, with no possessions, far from cultural pressures. Stripped to essentials, our inner burdens and negative emotions fade away. Out on the trail, there's a lot less guilt, anger, self-righteousness, hurt feelings, denial, and road rage to scatter our attention. When we remove these siphons, we once again have the energy to resume the work we were created for: the search for meaning.

Our natural state isn't hurried and worried, it's creative. Our mistake is being so busy planning, getting ahead, imagining happy futures, avoiding discomfort, managing our lives, and fitting everything in, that we leave no room for the inner pursuit of understanding. Yet we were meant to experience our lives directly, without overlays of judgment.

It takes a pointless activity, such as running in big circles for no other reason than running in big circles, to give us back the time to be with ourselves and free our minds and spirits to do what they were made for. That's why a "meaningless" activity like running can hold more meaning than entire days spent at the office, negotiating "important" contracts and managing "important" sums of money. For a short while, we've allowed ourselves to accomplish nothing and just *be*.

I began running again. Light steps gliding along the ridge, I felt buoyant. "Marc, where did you steal that line?"

Marc put on a mock-angry expression. "I might have added my own spin to something I read by Ortega y Gasset, but I don't call it stealing. I prefer the French term, 'research'!"

9

Running Solo—
Between Two Worlds

"Look at every path closely and deliberately. Try it as many times as you think necessary. Then ask yourself and yourself alone one question. This question is one that only a very old man asks. My benefactor told me about it once when I was young and my blood was too vigorous for me to understand it. Now I do understand it. I will tell you what it is: Does this path have a heart? If it does, the path is good. If it doesn't, it is of no use."
—Carlos Castaneda

If you ask a longtime runner why he runs, the answer is likely to be a bit cryptic, like the British mountaineer Sir George Leigh Mallory's famous answer, when asked why he wanted to climb Everest: "Because it's there." Ask a runner why he or she runs, and you might similarly be told: "Because I can."

These answers afford little insight for the outsider. The language of the longtime runner is the language of heart and spirit, which isn't the daily medium of exchange in postmodern society. The runner's response to "Why?" can't be constrained by rational linguistic chains; the answer needs wings. Spiritual flights can't be encapsulated in common language without endless attempts at further explanation. Analogy and description must suffice.

About twenty years ago, Rae Dawn Chong starred in a movie, *Quest for Fire,* that was based on an anthropological theory regarding prehistoric man. The movie gave an apt metaphor for the reasons runners run. It followed the lives of two men whose task was to tend a burning ember, keeping it alive so that the tribe could make fire as they followed the migrating herds. Lacking the technology to start fires from scratch, the men's handling of the ember literally spelled life or death for the tribe. Of course, one day the ember is accidentally snuffed out, imperiling the tribe. The two men set out on a quest for fire, searching for a new ember so that the tribe can survive the dark nights.

My daily run is like the quest for fire. It's a search for the rejuvenating spiritual spark that sustains me through the difficult demands of my modern day.

I live between two worlds, the material valley of the city of Walnut Creek, and the spiritual mountaintops of the Shell Ridge and Mount Diablo State Parks. A typical day begins with my dog Izzy stepping out the door with me just before 6:00 A.M. The cool air motivates us to start moving, but the arthritic stiffness of our still waking bodies limits the rate at which we're able to run. Izzy and I shiver, exhaling gray ghost-clouds. To ease the transition, we start by running downhill, past white picket fences, bushes of Olympiad roses, and Ford Explorers parked in driveways. We're trotting down the tributaries toward the heart of the material world.

At the bottom of the hill, we reach Ygnacio Valley Road, the main artery leading to the 680 and 24 freeways. There, I pass the first commuters making their early-morning way to San Francisco, Oakland, Berkeley, and San Jose. I glance into fogged-over windows and see grim faces sipping from steaming mugs, adjusting radios, talking with the East Coast office on cell phones.

As my muscles loosen, my stride lengthens. Passing several dozen cars waiting for the light to change, I think, *I'm fortunate to live close to the office.* I recall my gnarly days of long commutes, the monotonous five-feet-brake, five-feet-brake routine, and I empathize with the frustration in the faces I see.

I wonder: *Why do we put ourselves through it? Why do we tolerate losing so much time? What's so important that we'll spend all the days of our lives doing . . . this?* Oblivious, Izzy matches my pace, keeping the leash slack and sniffing the morning air. She lives for this. We turn left together, headed toward downtown.

I glance up at my office building, five blocks away, and find my window on the eighth floor, southeast corner, two stories down from the top. It looks dark inside, but I can just see the outline of my computer and the fileholder with my current projects. My thoughts turn to work and my customer's deliberate, relentless demands. Anger simmers in my chest. I resent the arbitrarily short Monday-morning deadlines, purposely set to "manage the vendor," ensuring that we must work weekends when support is least available, and designed to maximize oversight. I resent the signing of contracts in the dark foreshadow of negotiations opened three months down the line for the purpose of gaining further price concessions. I resent the coyly veiled and brazen threats to jump to other suppliers.

My mind races, hurling rocks at memories of past injustices, and I stiffen inside, realizing I'm not all that different from the grim faces I peered at through the car windows. I wonder again: *Why do we inflict this on ourselves?* At the same time, a part of me runs alongside myself, watching the anger.

I remind myself that in this exact moment, I'm running. I'm out here with Izzy—I'm not negotiating contracts, not managing crises, not placating customers. I'm not carrying my cell phone or my pager. At this moment, I'm running with my dog, and I don't have to bring the demons along. They're imaginary. But the basic questions remain, and they're valid. *Have we become so self-important that we'll tolerate nothing less than perfect products and services? What's so important about what we're doing that we can't tolerate a few bumps and potholes in life's road?*

These thoughts, I'm aware, reside deep in my marrow. They'll occupy me during many runs to come. For a moment, I stop questioning and take stock. My breathing is steady, my stride is flowing. I'm warmed up, ready for the miles ahead. Izzy and I turn left again, toward the main shopping district.

We cross the city park, its swings, slides, and sandbox quiet at this early hour, then pass the public library and turn onto Main Street. At the first of three Starbucks we'll pass, half a dozen coffee drinkers line up for their early-morning dose. We pass the Pottery Barn, Restoration Hardware, Eddie Bauer, Jamba Juice, Barnes and Noble, Macy's, David M. Brian, Learningsmith, Bang and Olufsen, Baby Gap, Crate and Barrel, California Pizza Kitchen, and Laura Ashley. Signs in bold red letters compete for my attention: SALE!, 30% OFF!, TWO FOR ONE!, WE HAVE BEANIES!—manmade electronic bacteriophages, designed to capture just enough of our attention to inject viruses of desire.

Even in the quiet morning before the shoppers arrive, it's too much for my senses to take in. As the meaning of the signs begins to register, my eyes rest on a royal blue Toyota Camry, its license holder proclaiming MILLIONAIRE IN TRAINING around a designer plate, DES10E. On the car next to the

Toyota, a bumper sticker declares, HE WHO DIES WITH THE MOST TOYS WINS.

I muse: *Is this our real destiny? Is this why we put ourselves through it all, to become millionaires? To win? Everybody needs a challenge, otherwise we suffer the fate of the lowland gorilla* (Lowland gorillas are said to have stopped evolving intellectually because they had a readily available food supply and no natural enemies—at least until man began to encroach on their territory.) *But challenge doesn't imply competition, does it? Even if it did, surely there's a line where competition ceases to be beneficial and crosses over to mindless or, worse, harmful. We need challenges to grow, but the aim can't just be to die with the most toys. There has to be something else.*

Izzy and I have found ground zero in the land of the material. The signs, plates, and stickers remind us why the city exists: for the accumulation of money. Money drives the commuters. Worship of the almighty bottom line drives the businesspeople; impels them to demand ever-higher standards of service and performance. And I'm not standing wholly outside the circle. Fear of having insufficient money drives me to work a job I don't love. *Why don't I love it?* A final question on the cusp of self-revelation sends white light through my skull, jamming the circuits. When it's over, I forget what caused the brain-short, and my mind wanders.

It's Christmas 1967. I'm seven years old. I come down the stairs to the most magnificent Christmas tree ever. The image of that tree, flocked with snow, sparkling with lights, and the amazing pile of gifts beneath remains etched forever in my memory as one of the great anticipatory moments of my life. It may also be the last innocent memory of Christmas that I can remember. Christmas 1967 was the year I got everything I asked for, including the electric football game, the magic set, and, most treasured of all, the Batmobile with rockets that shot out the back. Naturally, there was the usual less-memorable assortment of socks, underwear, and sweaters.

But I also remember that Christmas for something more. When the gifts had been opened and each of my wishes granted, I was filled by a single thought: *Is that all there is? I got everything I wanted, but I'm not any happier than I was before.* It was a bittersweet moment, liberating for an adult but terrible for a seven-year-old. I learned long ago that acquiring new things doesn't fill the holes in my soul. Today, I love visiting the mall or the downtown shopping district, not to buy but because I enjoy the atmosphere—I love watching people and feeling the energy. More often than not, I leave without buying anything. But for a seven-year-old, it was a scary proposition: *If a Batmobile can't make me happy, what will?*

Like a diamond, the question and the answer it enclosed regarding material wealth had many facets and colors. It's a question and a lesson I first experienced as a boy; judging from my present predicament, it must be time to reexamine it from an adult perspective.

I glance down at Izzy. At each of the last three intersections, she tugged me to the left. The cars, exhaust, and start–stop running in the city have made her anxious—too many unpleasant stimuli. The high country is calling her, and I, too, am ready for the hills. My sudden inner anger at my customers frightened me. All the books that tell you to love your customers (and they'll love you back) drift to the forefront of memory, and I suddenly feel guilty. Also, there's a nagging sense that I've forgotten something, some flash of insight about my work and motivations.

Another thought slashes through the inner darkness, like a coyote calling in the night. *We've forgotten something about our motivation for working. We're at dead center in the land of forgetting, and what we've forgotten is important.* It's time to leave the material world, retrieve a spiritual ember, start a fire, and illuminate this thought. Leash taut and straight, Izzy picks up the pace as we leave downtown and start back through the neighborhoods toward open space.

Once or twice a month, Izzy and I pass a blue-haired lady talking to her little dust-mop terrier and wearing a knit sweater. When she spots seventy-pound Izzy running toward her, her eyes widen in terror. Hastily gathering her yelping dog, she cries out, "Don't let that big dog get my Daisy!" We've played out the same scenario on at least thirty mornings, and each time Izzy passes Daisy without so much as a glance. Yet the pattern never changes; it's always the same trembling dog and the same panicky master, no matter how many times I've tried patiently to reassure her that everything's fine. Now, I can only pass in silence.

Leaving downtown, storefronts yield to landscaped gardens, concrete yields to asphalt, chirping birds replace noise, and a quieting of mind supplants the city's sensory overload. We're leaving a world where time is measured in megahertz, and entering a world where slowly passing weather fronts and the changing seasons keep time. We're leaving a world that values fast reactions above all, and entering a realm where there is inner time and space to contemplate and gain the measure of ourselves.

The sages of the world's religions speak of a reality behind the curtain of our everyday perceptions. They talk of a flow in the universe, and how we're either moving toward or away from God. They tell us that sin is the choice of self over God, and that we operate from love or from fear. They say the direction we'll take at a given moment is our own choice. I linger over these rich-sounding thoughts, but I don't really understand them. Izzy and I reach the park entrance, where a dirt trail replaces the pavement and the first climb begins. I'm aware only that the *direction* of the flow feels right.

I stop to take Izzy off the lead. Her body wiggling with anticipation, she breaks free and races for the nearest tree, marks it, then moves on to probe at a ground-squirrel hole with her snout. I set off running again as Izzy continues her explorations. After a few minutes she races hard to catch me, brushing my knee and speeding ahead fifty yards, then stops and begins her investigations anew. I hold a steady pace as we pursue our usual morning routine of catch-up-and-pass.

We run past the public vegetable gardens behind the Unitarian church, where tinsel sparkles from trees and fences, warding off the birds. Trotting up the hill beyond the church, the houses on our right begin to dwindle. Looking down into suburban yards, over wooden play structures, into kitchen windows, I see white tile countertops covered with piles of mail and magazines, and half-eaten bowls of cereal nestling in white porcelain sinks.

I imagine the lives of the people who dwell in these homes—their worries over mortgages, credit card bills, medical insurance, college tuition, retirement. Echoing my earlier insight, I realize that I relate to these people through my fears. I fear not having enough money. I fear losing the social status that my job and money afford. I fear not being able to send Zach to college. I fear becoming a bag lady—yes, a bag lady! Fears *are* irrational. Fear is the common filter through which I think about other people's lives. I seldom think about their real struggles—the people living in these houses may have spouses who are having affairs, bouts of alcoholism, depression, illness. I have no personal stake in their real concerns. Recognizing how my fears dictate my images of others' lives, it dawns on me that my fears dictate my own actions as well. And I wonder: *To what extent are my fears shaping my life?* It occurs to me that I'm not so very different from the woman in the knit sweater, trembling with fear for her Daisy. *If my fears are shaping my life,* I think, *I'd better start examining them.*

Ahead, Izzy stops at the first cattle fence, patiently sniffing the gate until I can catch up and open it for her. When I arrive, she adds her signature to the guest book of four-legged passersby, and I stop to catch my breath as I let her through and close the gate behind us. I take inventory. On my T-shirt, an inverted triangle of sweat has formed from my neck to my heart, but I feel good, excited about the miles ahead.

We begin the final ascent over the ridge that will drop us into the core of the open space. The last hundred feet of the climb are very steep. Walking would take less energy and be just as fast, but we continue to run. My lungs heave as we continue our step-aerobics ascent.

My thoughts wander to a talented engineer in his late twenties. Ted resembles hundreds of other young men who work for RadioGear and other tech companies. Ted's specialty is traveling to Beijing, Bangkok, Paris, and Tel Aviv to troubleshoot problems no one else can solve. He routinely works eighty-plus hours per week, including nights and weekends, and when he's finished he moves on to the next crisis. Ted has bailed me and my customer out on several occasions. He's the man in the TV commercials who stays in the best hotels and always gets the best airline seats. Hip, exciting music blares in the background as this man looks skyward, spinning arms spread wide, as if to say "No life could possibly be better than mine. All this work and travel! And I always get my free upgrades."

Ted is the poster boy for the world's talented, ambitious high-tech go-getters. He also has a two-year-old daughter whom he almost never sees. He was recently divorced. When I asked him why he does what he does, he told me he needed the money. When I asked if he thought it was worth it, he said, "I help people communicate more efficiently. That's a good thing, isn't it?"

The irony doesn't escape me now. I wonder: *If we can't even communicate in our most intimate relationships, how important can it be for us to communicate with people halfway around the globe while we're speeding down the interstate at seventy-five miles per hour?* The question isn't how much we're communicating; it's what we're communicating. Our willingness to deceive ourselves about the cost of our careers appears to be limitless. Some of us work in cellular technology so that people can communicate more efficiently, while some of us are working to avoid any real communication at all. From the outside, you can't easily tell the difference; it shows up in how we work and live. What bothers me is the part of me that's still attracted to Ted's image.

We arrive at the top of the ridge where I stop to take in the view and catch my breath again. Before us, half a mile of footpath winds downhill to the main trail that leads to the top of Mount Diablo—3849 feet high, seventeen winding miles away. The downhill provides a reprieve, and our strides lengthen as we cover the ground rapidly. Out of the corner of my eye, I notice that Izzy has veered off the trail to the left and is running straight down the hill, excited. An instant later, I see another dog, forepaws on the ground, head swinging side to side, tail wagging. She's "play-bowing" to Izzy, inviting her to have a good time. As this registers, I realize that it isn't a dog that's making up to Izzy, it's a coyote. I stop.

The open space is one of the few places where hikers in the area can allow their dogs off the lead, and the dog owners of Walnut Creek form a loose-knit, friendly community. We greet each other on the trail and occasionally stop to chat. Recently, stories have been making the rounds about coyote attacks on dogs and cats—for the most part, pets left out for the evening. Several times late at night, Chris and I have heard coyote attacks in the distance. A friend lost a Jack Russell terrier puppy to coyotes on her morning walk. The stories rush into my mind as Izzy, my beloved running partner, moves closer to the coyote temptress.

Scanning the brush, I count six additional mangy gray shapes in the shadows. All are about the same size as Izzy. I can't help thinking I'm looking at Vanity and her deadly canine sisters, prepared to devour my companion after tempting her with excitement and play. I don't see it as coincidence that Izzy's demons look like her. I call in a calm, no-nonsense voice: "Izzy, come!" She stops, cocking her head as the demonic vixen continues her devious frolic, smirking: *Come with me. It'll be fun!* I issue a stern command: "Leave it!" Torn between the call of her genetic heritage and the pull of an obedience to something larger than herself, she hesitates, swinging her head from side to side. On one hand is the pack, on the other, her human companion and guide, whom she must follow for reasons she can't clearly understand. Izzy makes the choice and trots back toward me. Leaving the pack for the path, Izzy claims it as her own by marking it before she joins me.

"Good girl!" I tell her, stroking her muzzle. When I look up, the coyotes have gone, fading into the landscape. We glance up the ridge, back toward the safety of the neighborhood. Maybe we needn't put ourselves at risk. But the drumbeat of our spirit calls, and we continue. We'll meet the coyotes again, today or another day, we know we'll meet the coyotes again.

The experience has energized me. *We're alive among the coyotes of the wild, and we haven't been devoured!* As we glide downhill, Izzy stays at my side.

The incident with the coyotes replays itself in my mind's eye as we run, and I think of the times I've succumbed to demons, and how this time, Izzy hadn't. My mind wanders to a customer meeting two days before, when a cellular network had gone out of service for more than an hour during the peak Los Angeles evening commute. The moment I walked into the room, waves of anger, frustration, and suspicion assaulted me. The customer demanded liquidated damages in the amount of lost revenue, plus compensation for the expected impact on the company's stock price the next day.

I had yielded to temptation, responding with anger, asking how the client could possibly know the impact of the incident on the company stock. We were talking about a great deal of money, tens of millions of dollars. Diving farther into temptation, just to show how clever I was, I added that if they knew how much the outage would impact their stock, why didn't they hedge with offsetting options? Heck, they could make money in the process. *Why bait them like this?* I wondered. *It's only making things worse.* But I did it.

Izzy and I reach the bottom of the valley and join the wide main trail to the summit. Twenty paces farther we veer right, onto a scenic single-track trail that runs parallel to the main route. Before us sits the immense scallop of Shell Ridge, named for fossilized shells found at the top, indicating that the hills were once covered by the ocean.

As we begin the hard work of climbing, I wonder, *What made Izzy return to the path, when I've succumbed so many times to my inner demons?* The mystics of all the world's spiritual traditions speak of the still, small voice that directs us back to our spiritual nature, and encourages us to merge with the consciousness permeating all things. For the Christians, it's the Holy Spirit. The Hindus call it Atman. The Buddhists call it Buddha Nature. New Agers call it the Higher Self. In every case, it's claimed that amid the din and bluster of the demons raging within us, the voice waits patiently for us to listen.

Some mystics have written about their conversations with God as intimately if they'd sat in the local diner and recorded the banter. Others have claimed to be channels for a four-thousand-year-old collective warrior spirit, possessed for the enlightenment of humankind. Others have spoken of burning bushes, near-death experiences, meetings with luminous beings, or divine revelations received during severe trauma. I have no such experience to compel me to believe. Inside my head, many voices dwell, a bickering chorus. Some are the voices of angels, some are demons, some are mere self-righteousness masquerading as moral authority. Some respond in fear, others speak in rational voices. But each really only serves to distract.

Isolating the small, still voice from the tangle has proved next to impossible, especially in moments of conflict. The best I can claim for my personal dealings with God is that I've retrieved the occasional, infrequent message that washed up on the shores of my consciousness in the quiet parts of my day—usually when I'm running. It's not a very reliable or efficient communication system.

I don't live in the world of transcendent spiritual experiences that others have claimed. My world demands that I pay the bills or face the collectors. I live in a world where I'm not just a spirit but a body, a body that must be clothed, fed, and sheltered. It's a world where diapers must be changed, on people who aren't always delighted to cooperate. I live in a world where even as I read about great spiritual adepts, I must continue to attend meetings with powerful people while I figure out where spirit fits in the agenda. The needs of my son, wife, boss, and customer tend to drown out the still, small voice.

I live in a world where, while capitalism continues to create an ever-increasing, insatiable appetite for goods and ever-higher standards of service, my MBA-trained mind can't think of a better organizing principle. So I run, because although I live in a world of material and emotional requirements that I can't simply ignore, something of the spiritual world has touched me and demands my attention and presence.

Continuing our climb, we wind beneath a canopy of oak past Bull Frog Pond. Oak leaves, laced with delicate ice crystals along their rims and inner skeletons, pad our footfalls. A cold breeze blows from the left and whispers through the branches overhead. A red-tailed hawk rests on an old stump, its head swiveling as we pass. The dusty sweet smell of wooded trail fills my nostrils. While my body works, my mind rests as the miles drop behind us. We emerge from the oaks and climb through open fields. Ground squirrels rustle in the underbrush, chirping warnings as Izzy passes. She remains at my side, tired enough to ignore them.

Leaving the meadow, we enter the first of five long switchbacks to the top of the next ridge. I glance at my watch. We've been running for an hour and eleven minutes, and we've climbed more than a thousand feet. The material world tugs and snaps at us, reminding us that we must return soon. The burn of lactic acid fills my right calf. The cells in my thigh muscles call out for fuel, and a hollowness has formed in my stomach, begging me to eat. A metallic taste on the sides of my tongue reminds me that I'm quite thirsty. But I am peaceful and happy.

As we reach the top of the ridge, the sun on my black tights warms me. Izzy and I stop to take in the view. From up here, I can look out over miles of landscape painted with the greens, yellows, and auburns of fall. Filtered sunlight streams through doily-laced clouds, illuminating patches of the city below. I can see my office building, and I can remember the lonely days after I first opened it. A BART train pulls into the station, and I recall commuting to my first real job. I can see the Garden Center, where Chris and I were married, overlooking the pool where we'd met. I see the downtown shopping area and remember choosing that special anniversary necklace. I see John Muir Hospital, and I remember the five-day adrenaline rush when Zach was born less than two years ago. I can also remember my mother-in-law's relentless grinding cancer, six years ago.

I look down over the rooftops of our neighborhood, and I remember the excitement of the day we moved in. I can see the school Zach will attend. I think of the tremendous possibilities within him, and I wonder what kind of a man he'll become. I wonder, also, what kind of a world he'll live in.

Here I am. I see triumphs and tragedies, comedy and drama—the entire wheel of my life displayed before me, adorned in sunlight and color, and I'm connected to it, and I am happy. I've lived in this town on two occasions separated by a decade, for a grand total of just six years, yet I know that I am home.

Again I'm overtaken by a flash of insight. This open space, this magnificent view, this connected feeling, is the reason for all the toil I see below. The real purpose of the work is not to die with the most toys. It's meant to pave the way for more important matters. Somehow, the people below, in some small way, have all paid tribute to this perhaps yet-unrecognized yearning within them. Through all their struggles, commutes, and dreary jobs, they've managed, as a society, to set enough aside to preserve this magnificent place where I and others can run in nature, sorting through our inner demons and facing the experience of our lives directly. We are physical beings, but we are spiritual ones. The physical, material world exists to support the quest for the spiritual. My quest has nourished me for today. I've received a spiritual spark, and now it's time to bring that sustaining light and warmth back to the tribe, to, perhaps, illuminate the sometimes dark struggle that we all face.

Even though twenty minutes of running remain before us, Izzy and I are really done for the day, and she knows it. From here on it's all downhill, with just two minor bumps. I glance at my dirty, worn shoes and feel like a warrior. I'm filled with the sense of accomplishment that follows a job well done. When we finish, we'll have run ten miles over difficult terrain, and no amount of bickering and politicking can erase that achievement. I'll go to work today refreshed and filled with the knowledge that the job I do really supports another, more important one. In this awareness, I'll be a little more accepting, and in some small way all of us will have advanced a little farther down the spiritual trail. But I also know we'll run again tomorrow, and the day after. Just as I know this, I know, too, that I have much more to learn. What I've received today is just a spark; it will need far more tending and coaxing before it can burst into flame.

As we climb the final small rise before we exit the park and reenter the neighborhood, I'm buoyed by my insight about the purpose of my toil. But at the same time, I'm overcome by a recognition that I've really known this for a very long time. Two years ago, we named our son Zachary because it meant "God remembered." It was my wish for him that he remember better than I. Perhaps I'm starting to remember now, too.

As we run through the neighborhood, a harried young executive rushes to meet his car pool, his red power tie flapping over the left shoulder of his Hart Schaffner & Marx suit. As he opens the car door, music from Jackson Brown's "Pretender" pours out. I catch a single line: "Caught between the longing for love and the struggle for the legal tender."

Yes, I think, *'the longing for love' perfectly describes what motivates the journey of self-discovery. We want to love and be loved, yet we're routinely told that money and career prevent us from being loved, and we feel trapped. But it's really just the opposite—our work supports the search. My real job is to carry the spirit of the running trail into the workplace, and into all corners of my life.* I smile at the irony of catching the line from that particular song, on this particular morning. The soul sometimes works overtime to manufacture coincidences.

10

Riding With Michael

"They were truly people out of time, but it was not that alone which drew me to them. Being a people to whom adversity was natural, they had retained a remarkable capacity for tolerance of other human beings, together with qualities of generosity toward one another and toward strangers in their midst which surpassed anything I had ever known before except, perhaps, among the Eskimos. They were the best of people, and I promised myself that one day I would come and live among them and escape from the increasingly mechanistic mainland world with its March Hare preoccupation with witless production for mindless consumption; its disruptive infatuation with change for its own sake; its idiot dedication to the bitch goddess, Progress."
— Farley Mowat, *A Whale for the Killing*

Something happened during a vacation that Chris and I took not long ago that encapsulated a dilemma that we all face, living in the machine of capitalism. It was during a five-hundred-mile "adventure travel" bicycle trip across Sardinia and Corsica, in the Mediterranean off the west coast of Italy.

Our adventure consisted of risking our lives for eleven glori-
ous days, riding through remote Italian and French villages
and falling in love with people for whom it's no effort at all to
smile, wave, and yell *"Bonjour!"* to nineteen sweaty Americans
dressed in tight-fitting clothes bedecked with brightly colored
armadillos and wrench-toting lobsters. We stopped in quaint
Mediterranean towns dripping with flowers and two-storied
charm and sipped espressos in streetside cafés. (I tagged them
"expressos" since I tended to become a pretty fast talker after
imbibing the thick brew.) We languished over three-hour din-
ners and wine, then slept serenaded by the waves, or our tour
guide Antonio's beautiful Italian ballads. Mostly, we laughed
from the moment we awoke until the last moments before we
fell asleep. But even amid eleven perfect days of picturesque
villages and self-propelled adventure, we weren't entirely able
to leave the dilemmas of progress and capitalism behind.

On the sixth day, I had run out of film, yet we never
seemed to ride through a town during hours when the stores
were open. We'd arrive at lunch, only to find the restaurants
open and the stores closed. Nor could we buy film in the
afternoon, since that's when the shopkeepers enjoy a long
midday meal and spend time with their families. Finally, on
the afternoon of the ninth day, we were resting beside the
road overlooking the blue sea when I said, "I don't understand how anybody makes any money around here. The
stores are always closed." Several others in the group agreed,

but even as the words left my mouth, I didn't feel right about having said them.

Carol, whom I'd nicknamed Carolissima during an evening of wine and laughter, looked pointedly at me and said, "I've got to get out of here. There are way too many Americans for me." And with that, she jumped on her bicycle and rode ahead, amid confused looks from some members of the party. But I understood exactly what she'd meant.

Partly what I loved about the Corsicans and Sardinians was the pace of their lives, and their relative lack of concern for things that keep us Americans busy. For example, making money for the sake of "getting ahead." Well, ahead of what? Whenever I was inconvenienced by the Corsican lifestyle, I longed for a shopkeeper who kept his store open. But if someone had kept an open store, I'd have spent money there, and if the number of shopping-minded people like me reached critical mass, the way of life we'd traveled halfway around the globe to experience would swiftly be eroded. All the shopkeepers would stay open to earn a slice of the pie, not to get ahead but to stay even and hold on to what they had.

How can a society maintain its quality of life, if there's always someone pressing from behind, eager to sacrifice a bit of their own life to gain an advantage over their neighbors? In America, we've responded by looking over our collective shoulders in a kind of group hysteria, and working ever longer and harder to assuage our fears and try to steal a piece of the dream. The Corsicans and Sardinians have responded with a social contract that lets everyone enjoy an honest leisure.

As Carol rode away, my mind swirled with thoughts and questions. The byproduct of our American approach is innovation. But have we ever counted the real costs of innovation? For all the devices we've invented to save ourselves labor and time, why is it that the Corsicans and Sardinians have more free time than we do?[3] These are really questions about progress and the role of the individual within the steady forward movement of society. The answers may lie in recognizing that relentless innovation comes at the price of our lives.[4] As technology advances, the stakes escalate. And even as they do so, we're rendered increasingly unable to see the trade-offs associated with new technologies, and we're increasingly willing to implement them without considering the consequences.

The Internet, for example, is universally hailed as the best lubricant ever for a frictionless worldwide economy, holding the promise of lower-priced goods and services for everyone.

---

[3] Many others have made the same observation. I first became aware of it as a teenager, when I read Kurt Vonnegut Jr.'s *Player Piano*. Vonnegut wrote: "The Shah would like to know why she has to do everything so quickly—this in a matter of seconds, that in a matter of seconds. What is it she is in such a hurry to get at? What is it she has to do, that she mustn't waste any time on these things?"

[4] Thoreau wrote, "The cost of a thing is the amount of what I call life which is required to be exchanged for it, immediately or in the long run."

Fast, easily accessed information, it's argued, will become the great equalizer, the ultimate democratizing force. True, perhaps, but the thinking usually stops there.

The Internet could just as easily become the ultimate weapon of colonization, in a kind of material imperialism that forces every Corsican shopkeeper to stay open longer or risk losing business to a faceless Internet company halfway across the world. And that isn't all. Today, almost every school in America has a computer room with connections to the Internet, which teachers and administrators point to with great pride. But if we ask, "What used to be in this room?" few will remember, unless an old-timer recalls that it was once a music room, or an art studio, or a drama classroom.

Liberal arts education and the pace of rural life will be just two among countless unremarked casualties of the Internet. I'm no Luddite; I'm not suggesting that progress can or should be stopped. Even if we agree that Americans spend too much time making money, and that the cost of some innovations may be too high, or that the short-term benefits of a particular convenience or pleasure are outweighed by their long-term consequences, we can't as easily change society. Not everyone will want to change just because one of us has experienced an epiphany. The only thing an individual can do is look within, understand his own motivations, and make choices regarding his actions while pondering the place of those actions within the society at large.

As we rode through the Sardinian countryside, I began to wonder what a more consciously balanced life would look like, in the middle of a society that embraced relentless capitalism. The next morning, an answer presented itself.

Chris was eight weeks pregnant with Zach. We had made our vacation plans long before we knew she was expecting, and after nine days of riding she needed a day off, so I spent the morning riding with Michael. Michael is a professional chef, and throughout the trip he would converse in fluent French and Italian with our restaurateurs, making menu suggestions for hungry bicyclists and exchanging culinary secrets. As we rode, Michael told me that trips such as this one allowed him to indulge his passion for cycling while stimulating ideas for new dishes. He talked about the conscious act of preparing food to please and serve others, and how his clients would receive his gift, his creation, into their bodies in full trust and faith. Michael considered the exchange sacred. Pedaling through the French countryside at a steady clip of eighteen miles an hour, I was hypnotized by his eloquent sermon on food preparation. I had never heard anyone speak about his work with such spiritual reverence.

Two years later, I happened to catch a commercial for *Regis & Kathie Lee,* and there was Michael, preparing a butterflied leg of lamb. Only then did I discover that Michael was a world-renowned master chef in New York. I'd had no idea, yet after experiencing his profoundly integrated spiritual passion and professional life, I wasn't surprised.

When work and spirituality become one, what happens? In Michael's case, a great chef had devoted himself to improving the experience of dining for the people he served. It amazes me to see how often the most energetic, integrated people live to serve others. Just as amazing is how readily others respond to their service-oriented magnetism.

It's all pretty low-tech stuff, really.

11

Running in the Shower

"Life does not consist mainly—or even largely—of facts and happenings. It consists mainly of the storm of thoughts that is forever blowing through one's head." —Mark Twain, *Autobiography*

Nearly every one of the popular hands-on science museums found in large U.S. cities has a gravity exhibit, composed of a large funnel into which you're invited to roll a penny. As the penny rolls, it circles in large, looping orbits, then in ever-tighter and faster spirals until it falls out the bottom. I sometimes think of myself as being like that penny, and that each loop around the funnel is like a new, more intimate perspective on the unfolding lessons of my life.

Important lessons must be learned and experienced from many angles before we can absorb them on the deepest levels. In the analogy of the funnel, gravity is the relentless pull of what I would call "love" or "the divine." But you could just as easily call that subtle attraction "truth," "understanding," "comprehension," or "God." I like the analogy because it implies there aren't all that many unique realizations in our lives, only the same lessons presented over and over again in different ways.

A common, unmistakable thread that runs through the fabric of my life is a deep yearning to get to the bottom of the funnel—to get closer to the direct experience of something unimaginably greater than myself. Call it my personal faith, based on the statistically insignificant sample of my life. I believe it's what we were all meant to strive for.

Only now can I see that what happened next in my life marked yet another, more focused orbit around the questions I'd been asking. I would see my life's lessons in a new and deeper way, as if for the first time. To facilitate the next gravitational orbit, Marc would introduce me to a man who was farther down the funnel, orbiting at a much higher frequency than I was.

For my part, I remain in awe at the unfolding mystery of life.

Marc said, shamelessly ripping off my line about a friend who drove the world's first all-Bond-O car, "I just read the world's first all-highlighted book." We had broken off from the pack of club runners, electing to climb a steep and beautiful single-track trail through oak-studded grassy meadows instead of a flatter but featureless wide-track route.

Coming from Marc, it was generous praise. Marc studied philosophy as a Wisconsin undergraduate and later as a graduate student at Harvard. In the ensuing forty years, he'd read nothing but great works. Marc wouldn't recognize a Sidney Sheldon or Jackie Collins book if he tripped over it. When Marc's college classmates teased him, asking why he still read Sartre and Kant instead of getting on with his life, Marc replied that he couldn't understand why they were running away from theirs by reading trash.

I had to know more about a book that had so captivated Marc. "What book are you talking about?"

"*Time and the Soul,* by Jacob Needleman."

"Never heard of him—who is he, and what's the book about?"

"Needleman is a professor of philosophy and religion at San Francisco State. I think he's a giant, right up there with the great ones. In his book, he talks about the notion that we're being lived by our lives, instead of the other way around. He claims that the starvation for time in our lives is really a famine of meaning."

I had an intuitive sense of what Marc was saying, but it was unfocused. "What do you mean, 'being lived by our lives'?"

"He means there are forces and influences in our culture that drive our behaviors, and that we're constantly reacting to them in automatic, unconscious ways. He calls them automatisms. I love that word, *automatisms*. Anyway, as a result of living our lives as a series of automatisms, life becomes meaningless. I don't know about you, but I could use a little more meaning in my life."

I had heard similar arguments, and my reaction had always been the same. Nobody wants to hear that they're acting unconsciously, myself not excepted. I suppressed the unconsidered reaction that would merely prove his point, and instead asked, "How do we go about finding more meaning?"

"Needleman suggests that we start by slowing down a little, because our relationship to time is messed up. We're always in such a hurry, always concerned about the future, always consulting the clock to see if time will permit us to do something. Maybe it should be the other way around. Maybe we should consider the meaning of an activity before we decide whether we've got enough time for it. Needleman also talks about how much time and energy we waste by imagining a thousand bad futures that never come to pass."

"You mean we're too busy hurrying and worrying through our lives to really live them, or for them to have meaning?" I asked, pleased with the rhyme.

"Yup, that's exactly what I mean. Show me a person who's in a hurry, and I'll show you a person who's worried about something." Marc paused, then added, "I also mean judging and fudging." Typically, he'd picked up on my little rhyming game.

"Judging and fudging?"

"Yeah. Always deciding that this is *good* and that is *bad,* when in reality, we have no idea what it really is. It probably just *is,* but we have to put in our two cents' worth."

"No," I said. "I think I understand the judging part, but I'm really asking about the fudging part."

"You know, all the self-aggrandizing stuff we do—giving ourselves credit for things we had nothing to do with, acting like we have control over things we know almost nothing about."

"Don't forget my personal specialties, avoidance and aversion. Alliteration works, by the way . . ."

"Oh, well, then the ever-popular plotting and planning must be recognized."

"Yup, and comparing and competing."

Our trail had merged back into the main route, but Marc added a final thought before we rejoined the other runners. "Needleman suggests that merely by pondering the question of meaning in our lives, we begin to find meaning. The question itself directs us. I love the notion of pondering."

I loved it, too. I like to think of the big questions of meaning as the stretching exercises that keep us flexible.

Over the next eighteen months, Marc and I would attend roughly a dozen intimate discussion groups with Jacob Needleman. My reaction to Needleman was a mixture of attraction and aversion. Clearly, he was among the finest orators I'd heard, but a part of him wanted us never to become too comfortable, too settled. I think it was part of his method. He would hold aspects of our personalities in specific relief, so that we could examine them more closely.

Needleman's personal search for meaning and self-discovery had been influenced by the teachings of G. I. Gurdjieff. Many aspects of the Gurdjieff work lay beyond anything I could verify from my own experience, yet Needleman gave me keys that I would find useful in my own continued search for meaning.

I eventually read two of Needleman's books, and I wasn't surprised to find that, like so many others, he'd chosen to divide human experience into inner and outer worlds. Needleman claimed that meaning comes from living in the inner and outer, material world simultaneously. I'd been approaching the same notion myself—that we must continue to earn a living and make our way in this modern and hectic world, but simultaneously bring a sense of wonder into it.

Needleman pointed out that as a culture, we in the West have no real tools or language that support the exploration of the inner world. The very skills that serve us so well for manipulating and managing the material world are exactly the wrong tools for navigating the interior world. As a result, any willful attempts on our part to manipulate the inner world will inevitably end in failure.

Early in our meetings, Needleman suggested that we try a startling exercise. He urged us to remember our feet when we took a shower. He said it was a way to begin looking inward, and to feel what it's really like to be human, at one with our bodily sensations, emotions, and thoughts. For me, it turned out to be a brilliant first step. The morning shower is possibly the last refuge of solitude left to us in these times. And the exercise doesn't take any extra time.

The first thing I learned was that I couldn't remember my feet for a very long time. It was a lot like when I started to run and couldn't go very far. Some of the people in Needleman's group grew frustrated when they realized this, but I had experienced it before, so I wasn't overly bothered. In time, I was able to remember my feet for most of a shower, feeling the tiny microadjustments of the muscles in my toes as I kept my balance, aware of the tactile sensations of standing on a bumpy floor in warm water. Just as I looked forward to running, I began to look forward to my morning feet-remembering ritual. But it would take a lot longer to figure out why.

Whenever I remembered my feet, I felt a deep sense of connection with my environment. It was a similar sense of connection and well-being to what I felt when I was running on a woodsy path. I remember a question that Needleman asked a woman in the group who, airing her spiritual credentials, had described several lofty experiences she'd had in her meditations. Needleman said, "What do you do when you get up from your meditation cushion?" The woman hadn't had an answer. One morning while I was remembering my feet in the shower, I suddenly knew the answer: You keep meditating. Why not try to continue to "remember my feet"—metaphorically speaking—when I left the shower and entered the rest of my day? A new and more encompassing spirit of inquiry began to infuse every aspect of my life. In a sense, I could "go for a run" anytime I pleased. Still, I needed help, and twice during our meetings Needleman injected a small shock into my search that gave me exactly what I needed, when I needed it.

After several months of trying to look inward and examine my emotions, thoughts, and bodily sensations, I became a little frightened when I realized that I wasn't finding anything permanent and stable. Everything seemed to be moving— thoughts, emotions, physical sensations, even my internal perspective came and went, forever changing. I no longer felt really in control of any of them, and with this realization, I was no longer able to define what I was. It was unnerving, and in response to my fear, I stopped looking inward for a time. When I presented Needleman with a series of logical reasons why looking inward was irrational, he simply encouraged me to stop intellectualizing and "just do it." And I did.

Needleman delivered the second shock seven months later. I had been expressing my amazement over the transformative power of attention, and how it turned the ordinary experience of taking a shower into something quite extraordinary, almost sacred. Needleman advised me not to become addicted to the experience of the exultant. He said, "Sometimes taking a shower can be quite boring."

Of course, he was right on both counts, and I feel indebted to him. He helped me learn that, in many ways, the internal world operates at a faster pace, yet under the same laws, as a lifelong running career. Sometimes the run transcends, sometimes the mundane overshadows. Sometimes the trail is steep and hard, sometimes it's flat and easy. Thoughts and feelings work the same way.

Needleman was right also when he observed that the *search* for meaning provides a *sense* of meaning. In my case, the search continues to unveil new discoveries, even as it moves in directions I'd never have expected.

12

Losing Los Angeles

"Things which matter most must never be at the mercy of things which matter least." —Goethe

Chris and I were enjoying a Friday night picnic dinner of wine and sandwiches on the amphitheater lawn with dear friends while we listened to Bob Dylan sing "Tangled Up in Blue." I'd expected the call, but that didn't make it any easier to pick up the phone.

SkyReach may be the best company in the world at keeping secrets, but I'd been tipped to the news by a slip on the part of a SkyReach attorney, months before the company announced its decision to rip the RadioGear network out of Los Angeles, the crown jewel of the North American cellular market, and replace it with a competitor's product.

The call was from my boss, who was responsible for the SkyReach account. "Dean, SkyReach just informed the Radio-Gear chairman that we've lost Los Angeles. George"—that was Big Jack's replacement—"wants you in Chicago tomorrow to quarterback a proposal to save this thing. He asked for you specifically, because he wants someone who really knows SkyReach. He wants you to keep him straight on what has to be done, and the proposal has to be ready by first thing Tuesday, when the corporate jet will be wheels-up to meet SkyReach in San Francisco."

I sat in an eerie, pale green spotlight, like the one the coroner in a high-profile murder case stands in while he delivers his autopsy report to a roomful of reporters. Like the coroner, I was flattered by the recognition, but I was also sickened by the task that lay before me. I said, "Mike, how many people know?"

"What do you mean?"

"How many of SkyReach's people know that the decision has been made?"

"The network vice president in Los Angeles informed his staff today."

"Damn. That's bad. Too many egos would be bruised if they changed their minds now. I don't think we'll be able to make a diving catch in the end zone."

"You know we have to try," Mike said.

"Of course."

I arrived in Chicago the next morning and immediately reported to George's office. After the meeting, I set about mobilizing the account team to assemble our proposal. I considered it a coin toss as to whether Doug or I would lead the effort. This time, I got the call. Doug showed his usual class. Supporting the effort without question, he kept the response moving forward, while I met with senior executives to decide on strategy.

As an account team, we hadn't been caught off guard by the SkyReach announcement. We had known it was coming, and we had tried to address the issues. But it takes time to turn a supertanker around, and, unfortunately, it was time that SkyReach felt it couldn't afford to spend waiting. In their eyes, RadioGear's software quality had hurt them badly and would continue to hamper their position in the market, just as the digital phone service was skyrocketing in popularity. Our team had put together several business solutions to address the technical problems, offering extra equipment and staffing, management for the network, and more, but we had never successfully justified the additional expense to our senior management.

This time, senior management was listening. They accepted our proposal to give equipment and services away, and they even threw in a hundred million dollars' worth of free phones to sweeten the counterproposal. In total, the package of goods and services came to more than a quarter billion dollars in giveaways. I had never seen the corporate heads behave this way. I guessed that, at a time when RadioGear's stock was already depressed, the company couldn't afford any more bad news.

I got another call on Saturday night, from Chris. Zach had been admitted to the hospital with an asthma attack and would be spending the night in an oxygen tent. Now, in a nutshell, I faced a central issue of our times—the trade-off between work and family.

I was in Chicago, working on the biggest proposal I might ever handle, and there was little Zach, sick in the hospital in Walnut Creek. Until that moment, I had always been with Zach whenever he'd seen the doctor. I had been there every day while he was in neonatal intensive care. (Zach was born premature; weighing just three pounds, twelve ounces at birth, he'd spent the first ten days of his life in an incubator.) I had held his hand through every vaccination. He needed my presence. But so did the proposal.

I work for a company that has won awards for its enlightened, family-friendly policies. Many RadioGear complexes around the country have on-site daycare facilities. If I had suddenly announced that I was flying back home to be with Zach, everybody would have told me, "You're doing the right thing." But the truth went deeper—there were written policies, but there were unwritten ones, as well.

The unwritten, unspoken code for senior management is unmistakable: Long work hours come first, everything else, including family, comes second. No one ever says it, but it becomes apparent in countless small ways. My career had stalled just as I was poised to make the important jump to the senior management. When Zach was born, I had begun traveling less. Instead of showing my face at far-flung meetings, I had telephoned in. I found most meetings to be a waste of time, in any case, and I truly didn't need to waste time traveling to and fro. As a result, I had more time with Chris and Zach.

But when you're no longer willing to play the corporate political game—cultivating "face time," kissing babies, and pressing the flesh—you quickly become an object of suspicion, a fact that's made known in subtle and blatant ways.

In my company, the top five percent of "performers" occupy two categories. The high-impact players, and the best-of-the-best are universally recognized as the "next-generation leaders." And as soon as I cut back on my travel time, my ranking fell. "You're definitely high impact, but the review board thinks you're a little too quiet to be a next-generation leader." I had accepted the evaluation as a euphemism, the veiled message being "You aren't putting in as many hours as we think are required if you intend to jump to the next level."

How could I blame them? If I suddenly discovered that I had cancer, wouldn't I choose the doctor who gave the appearance of being the hardest working, and who showed the uttermost single-minded devotion to my case?

Shouldn't the officers of a corporation exercise no less care in selecting the people who would shape the company's future directions? With millions of dollars at stake, the directors and investors would certainly be justified in saying, "Give us the brightest, most dedicated people, who'll bring us the highest return on our money!"

Does my experience support these criteria? Am I at my best when I'm working long hours for extended periods, or when I'm working reasonable hours and exerting less single-minded purposefulness? Many times when I'm out on the running trail, enjoying my own meandering thoughts, I've received inspirations for fresh new approaches to old business problems. Many times, the inspiration subsequently shaped the directions my team would take for months to come. And each time, the change of direction proved to be a more productive path.

On further reflection, if I had cancer, I think I might choose a hard working, dedicated doctor who had outside interests, who was curious about life beyond her work as a doctor, and who was open to the creative fertilization that occurs when we aren't blinded by obsessive, single-minded purpose. I might want a doctor who was sufficiently confident in her abilities that she could allow herself to enjoy other interests.

Even so, no one wants a surgeon who'll get up and leave in the middle of the operation. I had made my choices about family and work long ago, but I knew that, this time, I'd have to stay and finish the proposal. Too much was at stake. If I left the project now, all the doubts about my seriousness as a corporate player would be confirmed, and my effectiveness would be severely curtailed. As much as Zach might need me that night, he also needed an employed, unresentful dad. Still, Zach is the most precious thing in the world to me, and I didn't like the implication that the job was more important to me than he was, even in that moment of crisis.

In my defense, Chris felt that if Zach's regular doctor had been on call, he would have discharged Zach from the hospital. Zach's doctor knew about Chris's considerable care capabilities, and he also knew Zach's resilience. The ER doctors didn't know Chris or Zach, so rather than allow him to return home after the worst had passed, they played it safe and admitted him.

Chris and I, working as a team, had made the decision together—there was nothing I could do at the hospital that Chris wasn't already doing. We agreed that I should stay in Chicago and work on the proposal for at least one more day. And we promised each other that if Zach had to stay at the hospital another night, I would return and relieve her. In fact, Zach was discharged the next day, but I still wondered if I had just consented to yet another loss of traction down a long and slippery slope.

By Tuesday morning, after working forty-two hours

straight, I had ten copies of the proposal ready for RadioGear's chairman and his team. Just before takeoff, we decided on a last-minute change. While the executives flew west, I stayed behind to make the changes and arrange for someone to deliver the revised pages upon the team's arrival. Four hours later, I boarded a commercial flight home, drank a glass of bad red wine, and promptly fell asleep. The senior executives were wrapping it up at just about the same time my flight landed.

The proposal had SkyReach thinking hard. For a week, I fielded their questions, and as I answered them, I carefully pointed out the benefits and value for SkyReach. Then the phone stopped ringing. Perhaps we would pull this thing out, after all.

"Dean," Mike said, "we gave it our best, but SkyReach has decided to rip us." He sounded distraught. A picture from a high school history book popped into my head. It showed the weary, wide-eyed, defeated faces of German POWs at Normandy, soon after the Allied forces landed on D-Day. The prisoners looked as if they had seen the future, their stunned gaze reflecting disbelief that it wouldn't include a Third Reich. Now, I understood a measure of their shock. But another vision came: On a single trail through a grassy green meadow, I was taking giant, effortless, floating strides, and Marc was jabbering, on a roll.

"Mike," I said, "this hurts bad, but just remember that a little piece of us still goes running in the hills every day."

"Dean," he said, "I'm going to remember that for a long time."

13

Running With Marc—
The Beginning

"Until we accept the fact that life itself is founded in mystery, we shall learn nothing." —Henry Miller

Just the other day, one of my old work cronies said he thought the country was going to hell, and that the younger people had no work ethic. I told him he was out of his mind, that this generation is the smartest, most qualified, and most engaged to come along. I told him I could introduce him to fifty examples, and that I'd just met another one."

When I'd first met Marc, we hadn't talked about finding meaning in life. The unwritten code for men forbade it. But with rare exceptions, as when a buxom beauty ran toward us ("Is it live, or is it Mamorex?"), we seldom partook of baseline locker room banter, either. In those days, we talked about stock prices, what life is like inside a big corporation, and how the Internet is retooling the economy. But our conversations soon inched toward larger questions of meaning.

Marc continued, "I look at guys like you. You have so much going for you. You're hard working professionals. But look at you, you're way more involved with your kid than I or my contemporaries ever were. I never changed a diaper, and neither did any of the fathers I knew. When my friends try to tell me they were involved with their kids, I just look at them. I say, 'Who are you trying to kid?' I was there. I know how involved they really were. These are the same people who preach family values. I knew these guys when they were your age, and they didn't live family values. It's a fantasy they tell themselves to fill in the vast void of the time they spent away from their families. It's just middle-age, white-guy anger directed at the public. I look around today, and see a whole bunch of dads like you who are involved with their kids. I try to tell my friends that they need for you guys to become bet-ter. It's evolution, and we should be glad for it. I invest in companies run by young guns like you. They make money for me. At least, I know my retirement is safe."

It was a warm, sunny Saturday morning in December. Zach was eight months old, and he'd been "running" with me in his Baby Jogger II for three months. I spent so many hours away from him during the week, and whenever I could I'd pack his diapers, bottle, food, utensils, toys, and the rest of a baby's forty-pound support system and take him with me on my runs. For his part, Zach enjoyed getting outside, flirting with people, and listening to our conversations. I think he warmed to Marc as I had; he always seemed to be leaning over to hear him better.

"I'm not saying that your entire generation is better than we were," Marc continued. "But there are certainly more like you than ever before. You know what's different about you guys? You all have a high tolerance for ambiguity. That's the single most important skill for anyone."

"Tolerance for ambiguity?"

"Yes. The modern world is moving faster and faster, yet amid all the changing priorities, mergers, and acquisitions, you guys manage to get things right. Look at you. You don't need to be told what to do—you *know* what's important, and you follow up on it. You guys can think for yourselves. You can thank the women's movement for it. They gave guys like you the freedom to get more involved."

I reveled in the compliments, but a part of me understood on a more serious level what Marc was saying. My father hadn't been nearly as involved in my upbringing as I had been until now with Zach's. I said, "How do you know that about me? We run together, but we've never worked together. It's flattering, but how do you know it's true?"

"When I worked for IBM and Exxon," Marc said, "I only did one thing really well—I hired excellent people. I can spot them a mile away, and you're one of them. I know, and I can prove it. You let Izzy sleep with you, don't you?"

"Well, yes," I said, a little embarrassed but curious. "How did you know?"

"Every dog trainer in the world today says you shouldn't let your dog sleep with you. They have a line of bull about it, how if the dog sleeps with you, he won't respect you, and he'll think he's in charge. You've heard that, right?"

"Yes, I have."

"But you let Izzy sleep with you anyway. Why? Because of the pure visceral pleasure of sleeping with a dog. You're in touch with your emotions to an extent that you can see past what the experts tell us about dogs. And do you know what?"

"What?"

"Izzy is the best-behaved dog in the world, despite what the experts say. That, my friend, is tolerance for ambiguity."

A few weeks later, after a bad day at work, I asked Marc something I'd been wondering about for some time. "Marc, what made you decide to start your own business?"

We were running a flat, out-and-back bicycle trail through the town of Lafayette, along with the running club. With clear blue skies overhead and sunlight streaming through the trees, the dewdrops on the grass caught the light and sparkled back a rainbow of reds, greens, blues, and violets.

"I had to get out. I was being held hostage by my subordinates. They were always wanting a piece of my time to talk about everything except how we could serve our customers better. Most of my superiors were even worse. It seemed like all I ever did was talk to everybody except the people who mattered most to the business—the customers. I couldn't take it anymore. I'd fly across the country for a meeting while my son swam in a meet that I couldn't attend, and I'd resent it. I'd sit in conference rooms drilling holes in the ears of whoever was speaking, trying to feign interest, but underneath the table, blood would be trickling down my leg because I'd be stabbing myself with a Parker T-Ball Jotter to make sure I was still breathing. It was meaningless. It was time to go."

We ran past the fire station that backed up onto the trail. Outside, the firefighters were reseating the hoses on a pumper truck. Izzy stopped to drink from the water barrel the firemen had placed by the trail for thirsty pets. I took a short drink from the fountain, and as we started running, I wiped my chin and asked, "Was it difficult to leave?"

"A very wise friend of mine put it this way: 'A dog can eat only so much dry kibble. After that, no more kibble.' I had eaten enough kibble. But you really can't leave the big corporations until you know you're sick of eating dry kibble. Otherwise, you'll just wind up right back in the middle of it."

"What do you mean?"

"A guy like you, who's built up endless contacts, will have unsolicited offers coming in for ten years after he quits. People will be throwing big dollars at you to try to lure you back in. Unless you're completely fed up, you won't be able to resist the temptation, because the money will be too good. But when you're ready, you won't look back. You'll never be tempted to think you made a bad decision. I could never go back to working for someone else again."

We had reached the three-mile turnaround. We ran in silence for a while. I doubted I had built up enough contacts to elicit many offers if I quit, but I wasn't certain. And I understood Marc's point. But I could also see that I wasn't ready to leave corporate America. For now, I had enough to think about. "Marc," I said, "that dry kibble comment wasn't very politically correct toward dogs."

"Oh, man, don't get me started about political correctness. It's the death of all the best humor in this country. I already censored the line to be about dogs, and it wasn't as funny. You should have heard the way the line was first dropped on me. It was funny and appropriate for describing the situation, but I censored myself. Everybody is afraid to say anything for fear of offending."

I often think about Marc's comment about tolerance for ambiguity. He had talked about careers and sleeping with dogs. Much later, after I'd listened to him toss off many statements such as "The only really interesting stories are the ones that deal with ambiguity," I realized Marc was really talking about authentic spirituality.

Contradictions are rampant in spiritual lore; thus, tolerance for ambiguity is a required for the seeker who wishes to avoid going insane or painting himself into an uncomfortable corner. The universe is ever moving and changing. Hmm . . . but is it also unchanging and permanent? The Trinity is Father, Son, and Holy Ghost—separate entities that are portrayed as one. Many hands make light work; but too many cooks spoil the broth. He who hesitates is lost; but look before you leap. These sayings are true, but none of them is complete in itself. The questions themselves are like light, which behaves like a particle and a wave, depending on the apparatus with which you study it. Similarly, the answers to the big questions vary, depending on the perspective from which you ask them.

Some say that the universe is ultimately meaningful, while others say it's meaningless, and both parties, while arguing about it, can mean exactly the same thing. But the big questions also behave like light because they illuminate. If we want to begin to see beyond our personal darkness, we must ask questions, otherwise we'll never see anything new at all. But to genuinely ask the questions and survive the shock of the contradictions we find, we must be able to tolerate ambiguity. There are no infallible maps through this territory, yet authentic, conscious living requires that it be crossed.

14

Standing With Zach

"Everyone knows they're going to die, but nobody believes it. If we did, we would do things differently."
—Mitch Albom, *Tuesdays With Morrie*

Wild turkeys roam our neighborhood. They're my feathered alarm clocks, reminding me as I awaken that life is a wonder. I grew up in Detroit, not a safe habitat for turkeys, so when I see them in my yard, it's a special moment, telling me to pause and remember everything that's right about my life.

Zach is growing up in a neighborhood where wild turkeys roam, yet he doesn't need reminding that the turkeys are amazing. Among his earliest words were "urkey" and "gobbo gobbo gobbo," uttered in a high-pitched, excited singsong. When Zach hears the birds, nothing can stop him from going out to look at them.

The turkeys spend the winter months roosting in a tree five doors down from our house. When Zach was about eighteen months old, we went out to see the turkeys, arriving just as six of the birds were walking across the roof of the house, below their tree. Zach pointed and laughed, shrieking with delight as the big birds pranced across the shingles. Just then, the lady of the house came out screaming and tried unsuccessfully to shoo the birds away. Seeing us watching, she said, "I know they're fun and all, but they don't live in *your* yard. We can't use our deck anymore, and the skylight is covered!" I decided, *Turkeys are wonderful, but yes, I'm glad they didn't choose our backyard.* (Our dogs see to that.) I told the woman I understood, and she smiled sadly as she went back indoors.

It's one of the first beautiful mornings of spring, and Zach and I have finished our daily routine of bathing him and applying all the lotions and potions that keep his eczema at bay. I've been out of town for a week, and although I'm running late for work, I realize Zach and I have missed each other. I open the windows, and as we talk, I'm keenly aware of how much we're enjoying the sunny fresh morning together. Zach is pushing his arms through the holes of his favorite truck shirt, when we hear a "gobble-gobble-gobble" from the front of the house. "Turkeys!" he says. We sprint to finish dressing him, then he rolls over on the changing table and says "Down!", legs dangling over the edge. I lower him to the floor, and he heads straight to his miniature table in front of the window. Wearing an expression of intense focus, Zach pulls a chair out and stands on it, then steps onto the table. From that vantage, he can peer over the ledge and watch the happenings outside. "Turkeys!" he shrieks, pointing to two males and a female strutting across the street.

There's no question that it's spring. The two male birds have fluffed their feathers and are parading before the female with all the pomp they can muster, courting her affections. With tail feathers fanned like cards, the two studs resemble Thanksgiving crepe-paper pull-out turkey Hallmark cards. For her part, the female pecks at the grass with feigned indifference, rewarding her turkey-testosterone-loaded suitors with an occasional glance.

I stand with Zach, forearms resting on the windowsill, as he slips his hand into mine. Zach looks up at me and smiles, then whispers, "Turkeys," and his voice is sweet sugar to my ears. We stand watching the mating spectacle for a long time, and as we watch, I reflect on this moment, and on the events of the past week.

It began with a Monday-evening business flight to Chicago. My travel plans called for a quick hop to Detroit to visit my grandma in the hospital on Wednesday. She was ninety, and her body was giving out. After I left for Chicago, my brother Mike and sister Lisa boarded a red-eye to Detroit. Grandma's condition had worsened—she was no longer taking food or water. The next morning, I canceled my meetings and caught the first available flight to Detroit. Grandma's only two sons, my dad and my uncle, had died—she needed us, and for Mike, Lisa, and me, there was no question that we would be by her side at the end.

Trying to describe what my grandma meant to us is like trying to describe the worth of breathing. She was always there, sustaining us and permeating our lives. How can you adequately appreciate a grandparent who listened with her whole body to anything we had to say throughout our young lives, as if nothing else in the world mattered? How can you express sufficient thanks for the right wisdom, dispensed over many years, at just the right time, and for serving as a family's rock-steady foundation through difficult times? How do you repay thirty-nine years of unflagging faith in you, even at times when you questioned yourself? It's impossible; all we can do is be with her when she wants and needs us, at the end.

I arrived at the hospital in the early afternoon. Mike and Lisa were sitting at the foot of Grandma's bed while she slept. I reached for her hand, and she opened her eyes, and for the first time I saw a human being radiate. Her face brightened from within, the pillow and sheets around her grew brighter, too, and for a few moments I bathed in the all-enveloping intensity of pure love. "Oh, honey," she said, "you made it!" Until this moment, I had never imagined that a human being could pour out such overwhelming, unfiltered love. I saw it glowing all around her and between us. Later, comparing notes with Mike and Lisa, we found that Grandma had poured out the same love to them, and that they had witnessed the same shining. I wondered how many times in the past I had missed it.

"Oh, Grandma," I said, bending over and kissing her. "I love you so much, how could I not be here?"

We talked for a while, then Grandma dozed off. We all knew this was the end, and I was glad that nobody tried to pretend differently. My grandmother was a public school teacher for thirty-five years in Detroit, and I hoped for a final lesson. When she awoke, I said, "Grandma, you've given us so much. Is there anything else you want us to know?"

"Love each other," she said.

I had always considered my relationship with my brother and sister to be pretty good. Like most siblings, we'd had our ups and downs, but we had gone out of our way to do special things for each other. Mike had flown Chris and me to Thailand for two weeks to visit him. Chris and I had taken Lisa on a bike trip through Italy. We'd stayed in close contact over the years, so Grandma's answer surprised me. "Grandma," I said, "I think we do love each other."

She opened her eyes and stared straight into mine. Gripping my hand tighter, she said, "More!" then she closed her eyes and drifted off again.

We've been told so often to love each other that the words are drained of meaning; yet this time, coming from this person, they drove a spear into my heart. I felt a deep, literal recoil in my chest. I wondered if the admonishment, delivered with such force and clarity regardless of her weakened state, had sprung from the poignancy of the moment. But it wouldn't be long before I would begin to realize the depth of meaning behind Grandma's words.

Grandma had wanted to be home when she died, so our plans called for having a hospital bed and oxygen delivered to her apartment. Once the arrangements had been completed, she would take a last ambulance ride. After repeated delays, it looked like we were in for a very late evening. I saw the deep weariness in my brother's and sister's eyes after an all-night flight, and I said, "Why don't you go to Grandma's and get some sleep. I'll stay with her, and you can come back when you've had some rest."

For the next three hours, I sat with Grandma while she drifted in and out. We had but the shortest time left together. In the silence of the hospital room, I couldn't help thinking about the meaning of her life, the way she had spent her time. The inevitable question we must all ask ourselves surfaced: *If I had just one day to live, how would I spend it?* The famous words of a business sage whose name I'd forgotten crept into my mind: *Time is money,* followed by a wiser thought: *No—it's much more precious than that.*

The woman in the bed next to Grandma's broke the silence in an Irish brogue: "She's a special lady, your grandma?"

"Oh yes, quite special. She invested so much time in us all, I don't know how any of us could repay her."

In the same clear, unwavering voice with which she'd spoken earlier, my grandmother chimed in: "And it was worth every minute of it!" I laughed, surprised that she'd heard us.

Later, reflecting on the moment, I wondered why we'd chosen the language of business to express ideas that lay so close to the heart. Is the exchange of the marketplace the only common parlance that remains in our culture for the give-and-take of love? Have questions of career and commerce so permeated our lives that we must express the ocean of love and meaning with a bare teaspoon of words? "More!" my grandmother had said. But what did she mean?

Grandma arrived home after midnight. On her last morning, she gazed out to the patio at a bird feeder that I'd given her on her eighty-fifth birthday. "Ahhh, I missed my birds," she said. Outside, a bright red cardinal jockeyed for position next to three sparrows, while a squirrel sifted through sunflower seed husks for leftover morsels. Life continued around us without breaking stride. Grandma had deteriorated in the night, but she complained little. "I'm ready for this to end," she said. In a way that I found rather odd, it comforted me. *Funny,* I thought, *how a woman with no religion in her life could be at peace with death.* But she was. My brother, sister, and I stayed at her side throughout the day and well into the evening.

Before we went to bed, my brother, who'd always enjoyed a special relationship with my grandmother, said "Grandma, I don't have the words to express how much you've meant to me, and how much I love you."

"Ditto," she replied. It was her last word. Grandma was witty, intelligent, and spare to the end.

The two male turkeys face each other, five feet apart. One gobbles, then the other, each trying to extend its feathers farther than its rival. Zach laughs at the display. "Funny! Hee-hee!" he says. I love the simple way Zach tells me how he feels and what he's thinking, with no more than a single word.

Grandma's written instructions were straightforward: "No religious service, but people may speak if they like."

My brother spoke true words. "I never knew my grandmother to be intolerant of anyone. She had her opinions, and they were often strong, but she respected the thoughts of others, and she always let people speak. If she had one prejudice, it was against religion. She thought people rationalized too much under the guise of religion, and she was rather offended by it."

During the memorial service, story after story poured forth, telling how my grandmother had helped others in difficulty. How she'd brought groceries when money was tight. How she had formed a lifelong friendship with someone who was bedridden with debilitating multiple sclerosis. How she had looked after children for weeks on end while their parents tended to a dying relative or looked for work. How she had volunteered to work the suicide hotline.

My grandmother may not have tolerated the demonstrative religious, but she embodied the spiritual life of service. Her final counsel taunted me: "Love each other . . . More!" I knew that her life gave the answer, and that it had something to do with giving selflessly, but I couldn't grasp what she'd been driving at. Many times, my brother and sister and I had given to each other.

Outside, the male turkeys have begun circling, glancing sideways at each other and stealing peeks at the female. The female continues to ignore them and wanders out of the circle, dropping off the curb into the street. Zach stares, rapt. After a few minutes, the boys realize that the object of their affections has wandered off. They stop circling and chase shamelessly after the female, who has entered our front yard, not thirty feet from Zach's window.

My neighbor, Lance, the attorney, rushes out the front door, talking on a cell phone. His gorgeous young wife, Cleo, waves to him, but he doesn't notice or acknowledge. Lance is red-faced as he jumps in the black Porsche Boxster and accelerates out of the driveway, missing the mating spectacle. *I've rushed out the door the same way many times,* I think. *How much of life have I missed? What job deserves so much of our attention that we miss the comings and goings of the life unfolding before us?*

Lance and I have rarely spoken. The first time was a Sunday morning several months earlier when we'd stepped out of our front doors at the same time, both wearing running clothes. Lance waved as I ran past. When I returned an hour and a half later, Lance stared and said, "You ran a long time."

"Looks like you ran just as long," I said.

"Nah," he said, "I drove to the health club and ran on the treadmill. That way, I can watch the news and read the paper at the same time. I just got back."

That, I thought, *defeats the purpose. We spend so much of our lives hurrying, cramming in so much that we never experience anything deeply at all.*

Early in the morning after the memorial service, my mother and brother drove me to the airport. We were tired after a week in which we had brought Grandma home, said our good-byes, arranged for her funeral, and begun the long process of clearing out her belongings. I was anxious to get home to Chris and Zach. I woke up feeling tense and nervous about being at the airport on time. The next scheduled flight after mine wasn't for another eight hours, and I didn't want to sit around the airport all day. I was restless.

As we drove, my brother stopped at a Dunkin' Donuts. "I need a cup of coffee," he said. "Anybody else want some?"

"Mike, can't you wait until we get to the airport? I'm a little uptight about making my flight."

"We've got plenty of time," he said, closing the door and turning toward the restaurant. "It's Sunday."

Yeah, I thought, *easy for you to say. You're not the one who's going to miss his flight.* I sat in the car and devised contingency plans. What cities could I make connecting flights through? What would I tell Chris? Where I would sleep tonight? I imagined a thousand terrible futures, none of which would come to pass.

"I don't understand why he couldn't wait," Mom said from the back seat.

"I don't know, either," I said, anger rising within my chest. *Calm down,* I thought, consciously relaxing the muscles in my body and laying my hands on my thighs. *There's nothing I can do about it.* My agitation soothed a little, and we sat in silence.

My brother returned with three coffees. Handing one to each of us, he pulled out and headed toward the freeway. As he drove, he looked for a cup holder. "Where's the cup holder?" he asked.

"I looked for one when I got the car," I said. "I couldn't find one."

"There has to be a cup holder. Look again," he said.

"I don't think there is one."

"They wouldn't even make a car without a cup holder anymore," my brother shot back.

Why don't you just add the word "stupid"? I muttered silently.

"Did you look inside the center armrest?" my mother asked.

Of course I did. Do I look like an idiot? When did cup hold-ers become the pinnacle achievement and concern of western civilization, anyway? Thoughts and emotions boiled in my head. *How does my failure to find a cup holder in this car bring down our entire culture? Just deal with it, people—there's no cup holder!* I screamed silently. But it was too much, and I snapped, shouting, "Why don't you people believe me when I say there isn't a cup holder in this car?" As soon as I said it, I wondered, *Where did that egotistical response come from? Do the tentacles of my ego extend so deeply that I demand to be heard on such weighty matters as cup holders?*

I couldn't retrieve my outburst. It was out there and over with. I could only watch what was happening within. I looked at my hands, which I had relaxed on my thighs, just moments before. My wrists were cocked with tension. The muscles in my right shoulder were hunched. It was the same wild-dog tension I had experienced at the negotiating table with Big Jack. I was amazed. I hadn't cocked my wrists or hunched my shoulders deliberately, yet there they were. I had reacted unconsciously over a cup holder, as wildly as when millions of dollars were hanging in the balance. The same feelings of anger in two very different situations had passed into my body in precisely the same way. It was as if my anger had kicked off a computer program—once the program had started to run, I had reacted automatically, no longer in conscious control.

What happened next unfolded in slow motion. Right after my outburst, Mike popped open a cup holder hidden in the dash under the radio. "I told you there had to be one," he said.

In that moment, I felt a flashing of old childhood fears, of not being taken seriously, of not being accepted, of not being loved. I had just been found out. Fear that I wasn't smart like my brother surfaced and turned to rage. Inside the front left part of my chest, I felt a bony calcification that moved in a slow-motion wave from left to right across my heart, hardening it. I felt smaller, as if I were shrinking away from life. It was all so familiar and so foreign. Familiar because I had felt the same contraction thousands of times before, whenever I got angry, but foreign because I had never really taken time to observe it and experience it consciously. Then the contraction of my heart began to pass into my body, calling it to act. And in that moment, I knew. I knew that I had just witnessed the exact moment of identification. I knew that this was what the sages meant when they said that we act either out of love or out of fear. Fear is contractive, defensive, an unconscious reaction. Love is expansive, inclusive, a conscious result of attention.

Once I had seen and really experienced the computer program in action, and known what it felt like in my mind and heart, it stopped. The impulse to defend myself against my fears, which had turned and contorted into anger, dissipated by itself, and I did not become identified with it. I had done nothing but observe my own unconscious processes. I hadn't tried positive self-talk, or taken deep breaths, or used any of the methods recommended in self-help books. I had just looked inside without interference. And I realized that it isn't the things people say, or the past, or even our own emotions that hurt us, it's our defensiveness about these things that does. It hurts us physically.

Outside, the discussion about cup holders continued.

"I really like the adjustable cup holders in my car. You can get any size container in them."

"The minivan has lots of cupholders in it." And so on.

I was no longer concerned. I laughed out loud. *So this is what Grandma meant. Love each other. More!* It was too ironic to be believed. To love each other more, we must become more self-absorbed. We must take ourselves more seriously, observing everything that's happening within us. We must come to know our anger, and what it feels like as it passes into our bodies. This is how we shut the program down and begin to live an authentic, conscious life. The act of just observing ourselves brings light and space into our presence, and we stop behaving in unconscious, automatic ways. Surely, loving each other more means living more consciously. As we live more consciously, we can pay better attention to those we love. With one little word—"More!"—Grandma had told us that our ordinary efforts at loving each other weren't enough. We needed to work harder and more consciously at love.

I won't ever really know if that's what Grandma meant, but I know she felt we all bickered too much, and that she wished we would support each other more. And she was right. Life is too short to spend it suffering the meaningless petty rifts that divide families and friends. We all want more of both the giving and receiving of love for each other. Even after death, Grandma remained a teacher.

Zach and I stood watching the turkeys for another twenty minutes, until they finally wandered out of view. At one point, Zach looked up at me, squinting his eyes into little half-moons, and smiled. "Happy heee," he said.

"Me too, Zach," I said.

"Yeth," he said, in his wise, lisping two-year-old voice.

When the turkeys left, Zach went on to other important little-boy pursuits, like building block houses and playing in the sand. I was late for work.

15

Running With Willpower

"The hardness of heart of the educated."
—Mahatma Gandhi, *responding to a reporter who'd asked about the biggest problem facing the world.*

While cleaning out the garage one afternoon shortly after Grandma died, I came across the Gandhi quote in a paper that I'd written as a UCLA undergraduate in the spring of 1981. Then, I had understood only the metaphorical meaning of the words. Now, I knew they also had a literal meaning. I wondered why, after lying in the garage for eighteen years and surviving seven household moves, this paper, with this quote, had chosen this particular time to bubble to the surface. It's the kind of coincidence that tempts you to believe in synchronicity—that we're guided and shaped by forces outside our conscious understanding.

Just as easily as when we remove our glasses and see the world differently, we can put on new glasses and see the world anew. Chris and I went on a nature walk and saw no wildlife for two hours, then suddenly we made out the shape of a single deer, standing frozen in the tall grass. Attuned to the patterns that a deer makes in the wilderness, we suddenly became aware of half a dozen shadowy deer-shapes. As we continued our walk, we realized that there were several dozen deer in our surroundings. Had they been there the entire time? Probably, but we simply hadn't had eyes to see them. Once we learned the pattern, we saw it everywhere.

Attention is like the herd of deer. When you become aware of it, you realize that the presence or absence of attention is a central, defining theme in our lives. Many of our problems can be characterized as issues of relative attention and distraction. I began learning to view the world through the new lens of attention.

There's a five-mile trail loop that exactly defines the balance point of my endurance. When I'm fit and healthy, I can run the course without stopping or walking. If I'm not, I can't. At just around the halfway point, there's a hill that we affectionately call the Mauler. The Mauler is so steep that you can power-walk it as fast as you can run it. If I were racing, I'd walk it and conserve my leg strength for the steep drop and two long climbs that follow. But during a training run, the Mauler helps me gauge my fitness. If I can run to the top, my quadriceps muscles will be reduced to sacks of microwave Silly Putty. But if I've got enough left to run the two remaining long hills, I know that I'm fairly fit. And if I can finish the loop in less than fifty minutes, I know that I'm ready to race.

In a big racing year, I'll race maybe three times, and I like to choose oddball events. This year, I had agreed in a moment of temporary insanity to run in a twenty-four-hour, 199-mile relay from Napa to Santa Cruz. I was especially nervous because I'd allowed the demands of work and family to keep me from training seriously. So I went out on a midsummer evening to attack the Mauler and find out how far my normal base training had brought me. I had two months left to prepare for the race, and I needed to know if I should adjust my priorities.

The Rim Trail run begins in the parking lot atop the dam at Lafayette Reservoir and circumnavigates the reservoir through the surrounding hills. The 0.3-mile-wide dam is the only flat terrain on the course; the rest is steeply up and down.

I punch my stopwatch and take my first stride. At the start of a race, or even a timed training run, it's easy to get swept up by euphoria and burn off the first few miles at an unsustainable pace. A terrible price follows this kind of early indiscretion. It's known as hitting the wall, or, as Bill Cosby once called it, *rigor mortis*. First-time marathoners, myself not excluded, rarely understand that taking it easy in the early miles puts money in the bank that pays rich dividends later on. In my first marathon, many years ago, I let myself get swept up by the merrymaking of the crowd during the first few miles and ran too fast, naively unaware that I would pay the price of pure hell in the last eight miles. The race brochures had neglected to mention that my thighs would be surgically opened and hot coals inserted at mile eighteen, or that I was expected to finish even though the coals would burn with a steady, unrelenting flame the rest of the way. I lived to run another marathon, but the experience turned me into a cautious racer. I crossed the dam very slowly, then turned left into a canopy of trees shading the trail to the rim.

New understandings are a lot like road races. It's easy to get carried away by the excitement. People who've recently enjoyed success with the first stages of a new weight-loss diet are prone to babble about all the ways their life has improved, and all too typically they'll freely dispense advice for improving your own. But life's highways are littered with the bodies of failed dieters. Keenly aware of this, I remained emotionally neutral about my recent discoveries concerning the power of attention. Rather than rush to apply the "method," I simply watched my attention come and go within me.

The climb to the rim is long. At first, it's tolerable, because the effort is expected and your legs are fresh, but a third of the way up, a steep pitch brings the first darts of lactic acid in thighs and calves, delivering a blow to any lingering exuberance. As I approach this stretch, I'm passed by a young runner wearing black Lycra tights with blue side panels and a matching black singlet. *Not appropriate attire for this particular evening,* I think. It's still 87 degrees, even though the sun is setting over the hills. The runner's singlet is dry on the back, so I know he's fresh, but his breathing is too hard for this early in the run. It's hot, but I'm dry too, though my legs are itching, the way they do just before I break into a full sweat.

Attention is a little hard to define—I'm reminded of the Supreme Court justice's famous quip about pornography: "I know it when I see it."[5] Ask most people where their attention is, and they'll tell you what they're thinking. But attention is separate from thoughts. Sometimes, attention rides on bodily sensations, as when we bump into a bedpost in the dark. In that moment, our attention is on the pain in our big toe, and nothing else in the world. But sometimes, attention rides on emotions, as when we're feeling exhilarated or depressed.

I finish the steep part of the first climb. The trail still ascends, but it feels easier.

I'm amazed by how obvious the "attention" aspect of our lives is, and how frequently we overlook it. The gathering of awareness around ourselves is a prerequisite for even minimally skillful action, especially in difficult situations. To be able to say

[7] Potter Stewart, Supreme Court associate justice, *Jacobellis v. Ohio,* 1964.

"Maybe we should talk about this when I'm not so worked up," requires awareness that we're feeling upset.

More awareness allows more skill, yet we seldom deliberately exercise the muscles of our attention. My own experience is filtered through attention that's so scattered and diffused, it resembles a useless, vestigial body part, an appendix. We've all experienced a state of heightened awareness that's followed, just moments later, by attention that flickers, flutters, and fades. We're engaged in an enjoyable, riveting conversation with a loved one in a restaurant, when the television behind the bar seizes our attention . . . the pager goes off . . . the cell phone chirps . . . we overhear a juicy snippet from the next table. Hazy minutes later, we've paid the bill, said good-bye, and we're telling each other the time passed too quickly.

The time passed quickly because the meal and conversation weren't really experienced—our attention drifted away, never to return. The breakneck pace of our culture, with its countless stimuli that compete for our attention, conspires to make distraction the norm. I've lived most of my life without any real sense of attention.

I reach the top of the first long climb, and for the next mile, the trail rises and falls, trending upward and ending with a final, steep drop to the base of the Mauler. Some of the climbs are steep, but none is long, and after the first climb, the hills don't feel too daunting.

As I began to pay attention to my life, I got better at it. Just as, during my first months as a runner, I built up enough endurance to run two miles at a time, I could feel my powers of attention building strength and endurance through frequent use. But there was something more. In the early days of running, I discovered unexpected benefits. My hankering for junk food gradually morphed into a taste for healthier foods. Similarly, I noticed that paying attention brought a growing sense of ease in a variety of situations. Attention isn't a cure-all. Like this stretch of small hills, life continues to have its ups and downs, but with attention the swings aren't as severe, and the overall trend is toward an increased sense of well-being.

Reaching the top of the last small hill, I look down the steep drop to the 350 vertical feet of the Mauler. Halfway up the face, an ant-sized man in black clothes inches upward. On the descent, I focus on breathing long, slow, and even, storing energy for the crunch ahead. At the base of the Mauler, empty of thought, concentrating on my breathing to keep it steady and deep—in . . . out . . . in . . . out—I begin the hard climb. After only fifty feet of ascent, I notice that my mind is churning angry I-told-you-so's. *Why haven't you trained more? You should have lost those extra pounds. You're not a young man anymore. You'll let your team down.* Distracted and betrayed by my own thoughts, I strain to refocus on my breathing. In . . . breath . . .

step . . . out . . . breath . . . step . . . in . . . breath . . . step . . . out . .
. breath . . . step. Upward and upward I run.

As I persevered in my awkward but stubborn efforts at attention, some quite unexpected things happened. For one thing, I
discovered that there's a kind of nonverbal intelligence in and
around us, which we seldom credit. We're all familiar with the
intelligence of the mind—we can see the technological fruits of
that kind of intelligence all around us. We may question the
wisdom of eating of those fruits (some have even gone so far as
to suggest that the central question of our times is whether
technology works for us, or we work for it), but there's no denying the intelligence that contributed to their creation. It's what
we generally mean when we talk about intelligence. It's a little
surprising to discover that the same word can be applied to
describe how our bodies function. We brush an arm against a
hot saucepan, and the arm jerks away even before the burning
sensation registers. The body didn't wait for the verbal brain; it
intelligently knew what to do.

What I didn't expect to discover was that the world around
us possesses extraordinary intelligence, too. I recently watched a
television program about the latest scientific studies on the connections between things. A giraffe eats acacia leaves from a tree
on the African savannah, and the individual acacia tree immediately starts sending out a chemical distress message. Within
twenty minutes, all the other acacia trees in the area have sent a

lethal poison to their leaves, and the giraffe must stop eating. The balance between giraffe and tree is thus regulated. Trees that communicate with each other possess an uncommon intelligence.

I sometimes think the universe has intelligence, too, and that it sends us precisely the right events we need in order to deepen our understanding. I found the Gandhi quote in my old paper, for example, at a point in my life when it had acquired new meaning for me, years after I'd written it down. Life and the world we live in are constantly spewing forth wonders. So much more is happening than we can possibly understand, using the garden-variety intelligence of our minds.

More than anything, my growing awareness of that intelligence makes me wonder how any of us can believe we can control our destiny by controlling our thoughts. And if we did possess enough knowledge to control our destiny, would we want to change anything at all? Would a person, possessed of such understanding, pull the levers for material wealth and power? Or would that person ask for an even deeper comprehension?

I've reached halfway in the long, slow climb up the Mauler. My lungs feel like coarse sandpaper and my pulse is pounding in my ears. My thighs and calves are immersed in tubs of hot lactic acid and beg for rest. I face a classic decision: *Do I take the short but extremely steep trail to the top of the Mauler, or do I take the slightly less steep but longer route?* I want the pain to stop soon, so I take the short, hard trail. As I plod, my head screams about what a loathsome, detestable creature I am, and I lose focus on my breathing. I'm in agony, and I want to stop. I don't know why I keep running. Not from a sense of obligation to my teammates, or to a higher calling. But I keep running.

There are times when we're cut off from all inspiration and only willpower keeps us going, and this is one of them. Those are the most difficult times. Someone says something hurtful, and we long to strike back, but our beliefs teach us to turn the other cheek, so we force ourselves to try to do that. We apply pure, dogged willpower, not because we're experiencing love in the moment, but because we know it's the right thing to do. We've at least learned that we're better off in the long run when we refuse to give in to our short-term impulses.

I turn the other cheek to my cruel thoughts and keep running. *Let the thoughts flow. I don't have to invest in them.* I run, and a strange new thought steals in. *When you're on your deathbed, you won't regret a single moment of this experience. The hardest climbs are special. You'll look back on them as some of the best times of your life.* Where did that come from?

Grandma showed me the heart's deep-seated intelligence. Perhaps I was open to the experience because I was grieving at the time, but I haven't had another vivid, slow-motion conscious experience of watching my fears transform themselves into anger, then harden my heart and pass into my body, creating a formidable impulse to react. But I have felt the end results many times—the familiar, heart-hardening sequence that serves, since that day, as a warning that I must pay attention to my heart and my intentions.

Mostly, when I examine my heart now, I can successfully get out of my own way. If I stop lashing myself into a frenzy over minor or nonexistent stimuli, the hurrying and worrying in my life begin to die down. Sometimes, when I look at my heart, I'm even granted a boon, as when the minor irritation of cleaning the kitchen gives way to the sumptuous experience of water caressing my hands and flowing over the dishes.

Other times, watching the heart has helped me stop mindless behaviors that can cause real damage. Waiting in an agonizingly slow fast-food line, I examined the sensation of my heart beginning to harden in rhythm with my impatience. Just as I had decided to ease off the throttle, I looked up into the tired face of Celia, who was working the register. I asked how it was going, and Celia opened up and told me she was a single mom, working her way through school. It was humbling to think how I might have added to this heroic young woman's stress by expressing my dissatisfaction with the speed of service and complaining about the grievous personal harm I'd suffered by having to wait an additional two minutes. The least I could do was smile, thank her, and wish her well. In fact, the well wishing required no muscular, willful suppression of my anger—it was the natural outcome of examining my own heart.

Through daily occurrences like this, I came to believe that the real miracle in life is this: By merely paying attention to the state of our hearts, without interfering, our hearts naturally heal themselves, and float upward toward skies of well-being. With that healing comes the invigorating feeling of joy and liberation that a runner feels when everything is going well. I think of it as a natural movement toward love, toward unity. It's the heart that bridges the gap between how we think the world should be, and how the world actually is. The heart knows how to fight the postmodern experience.

The Mauler levels abruptly, and in two final strides I've arrived on the top—the literal high point of the run, where temptation lures me to think I'm done. But the downhill offers no relief, only physical danger. As I descend, my heart and lungs pump full throttle to flush the lactic acid from the climb, and my thighs wobble under high-impact strides on the steep slope, evoking images of a truck flying down a mountain pass, brakes squealing and smoking. I careen out of control, on the edge of falling.

Two and a half miles remain after the descent, including two major hills. A third of the way down the Mauler, I reach the community water tower, covered in sweat, and stop for a drink at the fountain. A cool sip, a slap on face and head, and a dab with my T-shirt at sweat-stung eyes, and I start running again. The last part of the downhill is gentler. Before I know it, I'm climbing the next long hill, and the doubts I thought I left at the base of the Mauler creep in again.

For the first time, I realized I was seeing things differently than the people around me did. I couldn't know what was going on in their hearts and minds. I often couldn't say precisely what was going on in my own. But I wondered if I was the only one crazy enough to examine my heart and intentions in the thick of a business negotiation. Here I was, talking about spending millions of dollars and wondering if my responses were coming from ego-driven impulses or the desire to do the right thing. At times, I felt like the white whale in *Moby-Dick*, one eye cast outward at the world, the other gazing inward upon my heart. Curiously, I discovered that the separation of vision didn't distance me from my life, but connected me to it, compelling me to walk more gently. I didn't talk about my experiences, but they made themselves known in small ways.

A coworker consulted me on a business matter, and I said, "Pay attention to what your heart is telling you." Yet though the words had become shopworn as they were handed down through the ages, they had a fresh meaning for me.

I heard myself trying to describe to another coworker the experience of eating a peanut butter sandwich with as much attention as possible. I described how the flavor exploded in my mouth like fireworks, then gradually subsided. Instead of taking another bite to light the fuse again, I had waited until I had swallowed and felt the food travel all the way to my stomach. I described how I'd realized that I often ate well past fullness, purely to satisfy my taste buds or salve some passing emotional hurt, and how each time I realized this, I required much less food. I had uttered the most archetypal California phrase ever to leave my lips: "I've never *really* eaten a peanut butter sandwich before."

My coworker, who hails from Chicago, looked at me as if I were wearing a paper pyramid on my head. He said, "Oh, I used to eat peanut butter sandwiches all the time as a kid. I can't believe you never had one." I thought: *This is crazy. Don't we all pay attention to our lives? Isn't our attention all we've got?* I voiced these questions to myself, even though I knew from my own experience that it wasn't so. *Maybe everyone thinks they pay attention, because they've never held their attention on one thing long enough to know what they're missing. Maybe we're unaware of our unawareness.*

I knew I was pretty adept at self-deception, and for a while I wondered if I was simply deluding myself with all these notions of attention, intention, connection, well-being, love, and the physical hardening of my heart as a signal to look more closely. My skeptical, educated mind longed for independent confirmation, some reference from the external world to indicate that I was on a genuine path. It would be many months before I would receive anything remotely filling the bill. Meanwhile, I continued making a sincere effort to pay attention.

Arriving at the top of the next-to-last hill on legs freshly filled with lactic acid, I began the very steep downslope, the first downhill steps hurting my knees. I glanced ahead to the second-longest hill of the course, its right-twisting dogleg face menacing. Because it comes last, it's often more painful than the Mauler.

Usually, we think of *paying* attention to something else. We pay attention to our thoughts, bodies, emotions, environment. We think of our attention as something that rides on top of these things. The more we pay attention, the more we realize that all these things change constantly. One thought leads into another, its flight path veering with a sudden distraction, like the choppy, disjointed flight of a monarch butterfly. We can herd our mind in a vague direction, but it's almost impossible to make it fly straight. And it's the same with the body and its distracting complaints. We stand still for a while until we get a little tired, so we shift our weight onto the other foot, and when we get tired of that position we sit down. But then our back hurts and so we change positions again. And once comfortable, we get hungry and so we go in search of food. It's like an endless relay where the baton is handed off from one complaint to another.

The body gurgles, growls, and creaks unceasingly. Feelings, too, change: Fear leads to anger and fades into calmness. In time, we realize that we aren't really in control of our thoughts, feelings, and bodies. They do what they do without much help on our part. But if we make the effort, we can realize that there's something about attention beyond the thoughts and gurgles. Sometimes, an awareness blossoms independently. In quiet moments, thoughts, feelings, and bodily sensations are seen as a floating bubble, gurgling and creaking as usual, while awareness expands, a much bigger bubble surrounding the littler one.

When awareness expands and declares its independence, we're still connected to our thoughts, feelings, and sensations, but we know they aren't the whole story. It's like jumping from two dimensions to three, just for a moment, while we watch ourselves from a height. From that perspective, we see how limited our normal state is. It's like trying to find your way out of a cornfield. All you can see is the tall, green stalks, but if you've ever viewed the field from an airplane, you can recall the shape of the field and the contours of the land, and find your way home again.

I make no claims to having made an independent, expansive awareness my permanent and normal state. I mention it only because I've experienced it sometimes, and because, every time, it suggested even greater possibilities within— important possibilities. These experiences helped me understand that we should do the best we can, within our limitations. That's the noble struggle. When all is said and done, we may not be what we've always assumed we are.

When I put my MBA-trained mind to work on the question of what we are, I think of statistics. We are a confluence of processes—of thoughts, feelings, sensations, attention, environment. When we say "I'll meet you at six," what we really mean is "Based on what I know now, in all probability, I'll be there at six. I don't really know if I'll feel well enough to keep the appointment, or if something more pressing will come up, or if my car will break down, or if any number of other things will happen." When we make a commitment to meet a friend at six, we're performing an actuarial estimate—we're guessing. Of course, some of us are better guessers than others.

Attention, especially attention to our hearts, especially in difficult situations, has the highest correlation to feelings of well-being. (I'm still talking like a statistician.) The food we eat, the weather, our health, and a million other things can affect our well-being, but the most important contributor to long-term well-being that I've discovered is attention. In plain English, the more we pay attention, the more a feeling of well-being infuses us. The heart is hard-wired to move toward love and unity, if we pay attention to what it's telling us, and if we don't become distracted by less important things.

I don't think the most important question for the twenty-first century will be whether technology will control us. Technology is neutral. The impulses of the hearts that create and use it might not be. And we can only learn about the infinite shades and moods of the heart through paying attention. Answer the question: To what are we attending? and you'll answer the question: Is technology working for us, or is it the other way around?

I've nearly reached the top of the last long climb. The man in the black outfit is somewhere behind me now, walking with his hands on his hips, red-faced and sweaty, two miles remaining to his car. At the top of the hill, I feel relieved—I've essentially made it, with about a mile and a quarter left to go. I'm looking forward to catching my breath as I run down the hill on long, easy strides. Three-tenths of a mile later, I hit the last little insulting bump of a hill. I had forgotten it. Feeling suddenly weary, I begin to climb again.

Life is relentless comedy. A blatant cockiness swells within me with every profound realization, and nature takes great joy in ferreting it out and slapping it down. I pat myself on the back and smile proudly because I've realized the importance of paying attention, and how my habitual state of scattered and diffuse focus is hurting me—and in the next moment I've forgotten to open the fireplace flue, I've locked my keys in the car, or I'm hunting for the sunglasses perched atop my head.

Even so, I must go on struggling. As Chris wryly observed, "You talk about paying attention, yet you drive past the trash cans and don't bring them in." I'd love to be able to report that, at the moment after Chris said it, I paid attention to the hardening of my heart and a skillful response emerged as a result. I'd be lying. What I did say was: "I'm not talking about paying attention to the garbage cans. I'm talking about paying attention to how you feel about the garbage cans not being brought in." An ill-conceived reply. There's a special application of attention, in which we're focused on how our actions affect others. This is vital. If we're ever to solve our communal problems, we'll have to be willing to walk in each other's shoes.

I've reached the top of the last small hill—now it's really downhill all the way back to parking lot. I drop along the plunging ridgeline, and the chirping crickets all around fall quiet as I pass, creating a five-foot circle of silence that moves with me. I'm struck by the views over the Lafayette Reservoir and beyond to Mount Diablo. It's a moment beyond description, in which everything feels perfect, and I stop to take it in. The trees are sitting just right, the wind rustling through the pines. The birds are flittering about, singing their sweet songs. The water reflects the evening sky. After a minute of standing and looking at perfection, I hear the sound of sleigh bells, faint at first but growing louder. The next thing I know, a yellow Lab with a collar of Christmas bells comes bounding out of the weeds. He approaches me and then sits facing the view, nuzzling his head under my hand. We look outward together for a while, then for no reason that I can discern the dog gets up and disappears into the brush, the bells growing fainter as he draws away.

It strikes me that all life is like that dog. Events pulse out of the void, reach full aperture, and fade away back into the emptiness—like the waves that Richard pointed out, long ago. Thoughts, feelings, sensations, and mysterious yellow Labradors with bells arrive, and the experiences are made of the same stuff. They come from the same ocean of life, just perfect. I don't know how else to describe it. I never saw the dog again, but I think of him sometimes when a coworker enters my office door with a problem, or an old friend calls out of the blue, or I get a flat tire. All life is the pulsing of yellow Labs in and out of our experience. Maybe the only questions we should ask are: Do we realize how unique the encounter is? Are we really experiencing it? Or are we letting ourselves be distracted by something else?

Invigorated, I sprint the final downhill half mile through the picnic area, reaching the parking lot and punching my stopwatch. I take a drink and allow myself to cool down, then I look at my time: fifty minutes, one second, including a few moments of eternity with a mysterious yellow dog. I can't predict how I'll perform on race day, but I know the honest effort is good enough.

16

Running With the Club

"Do the thing and you will have the power, but they that do not the thing have not the power." —Ralph Waldo Emerson

On a Saturday morning in early fall, Marc and I set out with the president of the running club, affectionately called Double-Oh-Seven because his last name is Bond. Born with one arm, employed as an airline mechanic, and by all accounts the best in the business, 007 exudes the quiet determination of a man who's squarely faced and overcome significant hurdles. 007 once told me, "I'm a little sensitive about people saying they can't do something for one imaginary reason or another." On a competitive run or bike ride, one quickly appreciates how fit he is. His motto is: "Death before DNF"—Did Not Finish.

As we ran, Marc began a stream-of-consciousness binge while 007 and I enjoyed the ride. Marc talked about the wonderful California weather and wondered aloud why anyone would choose to live in the Midwest. Marc is from Wisconsin, I grew up in Michigan, and 007 is from Ohio. Marc glanced up at Mount Diablo and remarked on how flat the Midwest is. 007 and I obliged by asking in unison, "How flat is it?"

"It's so flat, when your dog runs away, you can see him for three days," Marc quipped.

"Material so old, it's fresh again," I teased.

Without pausing, Marc suggested that the weather in the Midwest is "colder than a mother-in-law's embrace," and then smoothly segued to politics and life in America.

We ran on, laughing and listening. After a solid twenty minutes of Marc's soliloquizing, Nic, dubbed Knee-Coh-Liss in a poor imitation of his Peruvian accent, ran past us with Jim, called Jayhawk because he attended the University of Kansas thirty-five years before. Without pausing, Marc continued: "Take Knee-Koh-Liss here, he thinks living in America is all about starting your own business and getting ahead by making lots of money." Which was exactly what Nic had accomplished.

"What is America about?" I asked.

"It's about riding your bicycle," 007 chimed in.

I laughed, knowing exactly what he meant. We live in a country that since its very inception has held that the individual's pursuit of happiness is an inalienable right, and backs that belief by granting its citizens tremendous individual freedoms. The question left to us is: How do we undertake such pursuit? 007 finds happiness, and meaning, by riding his bicycle.

Marc continued, "Now, take Jayhawk here, he got out while the getting is good."

Jim had spent twenty-eight years working for Chevron. When the company instituted more than half a dozen waves of layoffs during the 1990s, it offered early-retirement packages to hold down "involuntary separations." I spent ten years at Chevron, leaving for business school just before the "rightsizing" began. Having many friends in common with Jim, I knew what a traumatic, soul-searching time it was, even for those who managed to keep their jobs. "Big companies," Jim once told me when we discussed the situation, "prey on fear. They want you to believe you can't get by without them, but they're wrong." Jim took the retirement package without regrets, and he'd never looked back. Early retirement gave him the opportunity he'd always wanted to train hard and become a triathlete, a plan that had netted him two Hawaiian Ironman finishes.

Marc went on: "While his former Chevron compatriots are fighting for the next promotion or next raise, Jayhawk has his feet on the dashboard, living the dream and planning his next triathlon. Of course, these days everybody wants what Jim has already got. It's the hot thing to be able to put 'Ironman finisher' on your résumé. All these Silicon Valley instant millionaires get their mansions and Ferraris, then they look around and see that everyone's doing the same thing. They realize there's nothing they can buy that their dotcom neighbors can't afford, so they go looking for something they can put on their résumés that everybody else doesn't have. And they come up with the idea of running in an Ironman. Of course, when I go to hire somebody, I want a chain smoker with a cholesterol count of three hundred. I don't want someone who's itching to leave the office to go for a run. I want somebody who's willing to ignore his family and put his life on hold for my business. So, Dean, when are you going to get out of corporate America and put your feet up?"

I said, "I still have Zach's college education to pay for. I can't afford to quit."

"Dean, just remember, no kid ever grew up and said 'My dad spent a lot of time with me, but he sure was a deadbeat because he didn't pay for my college education.' Can you imagine being a kid like Zach, growing up in a home where both parents are active and involved and leading fulfilling lives? You and Chris won't try to live your lives through Zach, because you've got lives of your own. When you go to a swim meet, you can be interested but not concerned. You'll understand the importance of his participation, but you won't care if he wins or loses. Zach won't ever suffer the public humiliation of parents who don't like themselves and who try to live through the accomplishments of their children. Of course, don't expect Zach to appreciate this, because he won't, at least not until he's well grown."

We passed Meagan, who'd broken up with her boyfriend of nine years. Her demeanor reflected devastation and loss. I'd observed Marc talking to her before the run. She'd looked happier after they'd spoken, but now her shoulders were stooped again, and her usually fluid stride seemed tentative. After we passed, Marc said, "To borrow Dean's phrase, we've got to start pumping up Meagan's tennis shoes. Can you imagine a smart, athletic, good-looking, smoky motor scooter like that being crushed by a guy? It almost makes me embarrassed to carry a Y chromosome. If I were young and single, I'd be all over her like a duck on a June bug. Yet there she is, wrecked by a guy who from the beginning said he had no interest in marriage. Therein lies the evil in predicating your life on somebody else."

007 chimed in, "You know the stereotype about women tending to identify with their families and relationships, and men tending to identify with their jobs."

As soon as he'd said it, I realized it was exactly what I'd been doing for the last several years. I'd been identifying with my job, and now I was in the process of extracting my personal identity.

Just past four and a half miles, we reached the longest climb of the run, six hundred vertical feet in less than a mile, then back down half a mile to the parking lot. Even Marc stopped talking. Once over the top, Alan caught us on the downhill. "That hill gets tougher every time," he said.

"That hill," I said, "is the best part of your day."

"What do you mean?" Alan asked, surprised.

"Because we can do it, and most people aren't that lucky. Climbing that hill is the culmination of years of training. People are starved for a sense of self-worth, and they'll do all kinds of things to satiate that hunger. But not us—we have hills to challenge ourselves and remind us we're still alive. Getting to the top is your accomplishment, not anybody else's. Nothing will ever erase that accomplishment. No amount of politicking by anybody is going to take away the fact that you got yourself up here. Not many things in life work that way."

Marc said, "And no amount of genuflecting."

I said, "And no amount of butt kissing."

"No amount of kowtowing," Marc said.

"No amount of prostrating onself."

Alan looked as if he'd swallowed a fly. Clearly, he didn't know what to make of us. Marc, 007, and I laughed as we glided down the final half mile to the parking lot.

17

Marc and the Tarantula

"No longer conscious of my movement, I discovered a new unity with nature. I had found a new source of power and beauty, a source I never dreamt existed."
—Roger Bannister, *on breaking the four-minute mile.*

On an early-fall morning, Marc and I set out on a meandering run through the Shell Ridge Open Space. I had begun to tell Marc about an interesting call I'd received. A customer from SkyReach had called to complain about the quality of service they were receiving from the company that had replaced us in the Los Angeles market.

As I related the story, halfway up a two-mile climb, a tarantula made its slow progress across our path, extending one hairy-knuckled leg at a time. Marc and I stopped to watch its advance, and I was grateful for the rest. A fine specimen, one of the largest I'd seen, with a body the size of a fifty-cent piece and a leg radius bigger than the palm of my hand.

As we watched, I told Marc, "I used to be just like that spider—but now, not as much."

"What do you mean?"

"It's fall, and the eligible male tarantulas, after seven years of perfectly happy bachelorhood, are leaving their holes in search of female companionship. But here's the rub: When he finds a female tarantula, if she finds him unacceptable, she'll eat him. If she thinks he's one attractive hunk of a hairy tarantula, they'll mate, but then she'll kick him out and he'll die in the cold night. Either way, the guy is literally walking toward his death."

Marc, hands on his knees, raised his head and looked straight into my eyes and smiled. "So you're saying you're no longer like this spider, because there's no chance you'll get lucky tonight?"

"That may or may not be true." I smiled back. "But that isn't where I was going. This tarantula is literally turning his life over to his job. I'm saying I used to do that. I'd rise with every success and fall with every setback. Now, not as much."

"Go on," Marc said, as he started to run again.

"I was telling you how I got a call from someone who said SkyReach is having the same problems with our competitors that they had with us. The caller said, 'You're probably glad to hear it, Dean.' The truth is, I was a *little* glad to hear it, but I mostly really wanted SkyReach to be successful."

We reached the first set of switchbacks, just below a water

tower where we would traverse a shoulder on our way to the top. Marc said, "What's different now?"

"You have to know some history to understand what I'm about to say. When I was a senior in high school, I was captain of the swim team, and I was convinced I could make the Olympic team. That year, I completely dedicated myself to swimming, no holds barred. I worked out six hours a day.

"Early in the season, we had a meet with the local Catholic high school, which had two All-American state champions. I raced them both that night, and I lost both races by a combined eight one-hundredths of a second. The difference of a blink of an eye for two races. But I had made up a lot of ground to get even that close, and I was pretty confident I could beat them at the state championships.

"Anyway, my coach had to leave town over the Christmas holidays, and he arranged for us to work out with the team at this Catholic high school in his absence. Meanwhile, I had become a workout animal, and I got in the pool every day with these two guys who'd barely beaten me a month earlier, and I just punished them. I mean, I didn't let them beat me to the wall on any repeat, in any set, in any practice. It got so bad, they started taking turns leading off against me, so they could rest on every other repeat and switch off racing me. But it didn't work—by the end of the holiday break, I was in their heads. I knew it, and they knew I knew it."

"What happened?" Marc asked.

"I knew there were more gifted swimmers in the world than me—just look at how short my arms are, and how small my hands are. But I was convinced that I could work harder than anybody and win. I didn't even warm up slow anymore—I never let up. I just knew that if I worked hard enough, and if I wanted it bad enough, I was going to win." I grew silent for a while, breathing deeply as we continued the climb.

"Okay, I can understand that. So what has that got to do with your customer calling?"

"For a long time, I took the same attitude of 'work harder than anyone and punish the competition' to my job. When it looked as if we wouldn't win a contract, I'd try to make it as painful as possible for the competition, so they'd think twice before trying to encroach again on what I considered my territory. Formerly, if a customer had told me that my competition had stumbled in L.A., I would have rejoiced."

"What's changed?"

"The end of the story about my high school swimming career is that by the end of the season I simply broke down under the workload. I ended up in the hospital with mononucleosis and hepatitis, and I watched those two guys win their events on television. What's changed is that I don't dwell on the great workouts anymore, because I remember the bigger picture. When my customer called, I felt bad that SkyReach was having troubles. We need them to succeed in all their markets, even where we're not the supplier, because it's good for everybody.

"The point is, there are times to compete, and times to let go. If I'd known this in high school, I might have stayed healthy. Just recently, I came to the conclusion that the same thing applies to work. We can compete in L.A. again if we come up with an innovative new idea. Right now, though, we're not going to get L.A. back no matter how unhappy the customer is, or how much I rejoice about it. It's just too expensive for the customer to switch back to us. And besides, it would be too embarrassing for them to come back to us. We blew it when we had them, and we need to retool to live and compete another day. The point is, unlike the male tarantula, I don't have to identify so closely with my work that I let it consume me."

Marc said, "It's a bit of a stretch to tie it to the spider. The spider does his thing to fulfill the greater purpose of perpetuating the future of spiders. You don't."

"I know it's a stretch, but it makes sense to my mind. The difference between humans and tarantulas is that human beings can choose, at least nominally, how much of themselves they'll give over to their work. The trouble is, most of us forget that, and we get lost anyway. I know."

18

Marc and the Mountain

"To discover a metaphysical relationship of Quality and the Buddha at some mountaintop of personal experience is very spectacular. And very unimportant. If that were all this Chautauqua was about I should be dismissed. What's important is the relevance of such a discovery to all the valleys of this world, and all the dull, dreary jobs and monotonous years that await all of us in them."
—Robert Pirsig, *Zen and the Art of Motorcycle Maintenance*

The October dawn broke cool and clear, perfect for the task at hand. Marc and I had decided to run a half marathon to the top of 3849-foot Mount Diablo. The run began at the local high school, altitude 149 feet. Just 3700 vertical feet and thirteen miles to the finish line. Marc had run to the summit many times, but this was my first attempt. Fear and doubt churned in the nervous waters of my stomach. During the last two years, I had occasionally thought about trying the run, and this was the morning.

"Look at the bright side," I joked. "At least there's just one hill."

"We'll start slow," Marc replied, "and we'll taper off." (Marc and I had each separately met Walt Stack, the legendary Bay Area runner who had authored that famous line, which is now widely quoted among runners.)

Old running jokes provided a comfortable distraction from the awesome task ahead. For the first six miles, we climbed steadily in a pack of about a dozen runners while Marc rambled off on a soliloquy. "What a privilege it is to live here and do this," he said. "Can you think of a single thing you'd rather be doing?"

I felt expansive—brain swelling with endorphins, I was prepared to embrace the whole world and declare my love. "Marc, why *don't* more people do this?"

"Effort," Marc said, as we approached the Bar AK ranch, loped around a corner, and headed up another steep pitch. "People are afraid of effort. They think it's just plain easier not to make an effort."

"Yes, but there are so few things in this world you can point to and say 'This makes life better.' Running improves your diet, your health, and your mood. You feel good about yourself, and you feel more energetic and alive. And I often get the fringe benefit of listening to you pontificate." We cleared the steep pitch and approached Turtle Rock, which I think resembles a stegosaurus more than a turtle. "Why is it some people do this, and others don't?"

"In *Zen and the Art of Motorcycle Maintenance,* Robert

Pirsig calls metaphysics 'the high country of the mind.' It takes a lot of effort to get to the high country, and even more effort to stay there once you've arrived, but it's worth it. Pirsig would say that unless you make the effort, you'll remain in the same valley of thought your whole life. You can't move to a new valley of thought without going over high country. You just said the same thing about the effort that's required to live a running lifestyle. You can't really tell a person how much better it feels when you're fit. They've got to experience it for themselves. But it requires effort. Most people think they're too busy to run, or they can't imagine that life could feel different than it does. They have no idea what they're missing."

I thought: *The same could be said about attention.*

As we mounted the ridgelines of the foothills, Marc and I pulled away from the other runners. On the steep pitches, only the wind and our breathing broke the silence, and on the softer sections we talked. When a stretch of road turned north into the teeth of the wind, we began switching off the lead, giving the runner in the lee a brief, welcome rest.

"What have you been thinking about lately?" Marc asked.

I enjoyed the question. Marc and I had spent two years on a journey of earnest self-discovery, and the question presupposed a respect for our joint quest. More, it reinforced a feeling that I was not alone. We reached the Mount Diablo Ranger Station at 8.6 miles, which I consider the halfway point, since the last 4.5 miles are very steep, with poor protection from the wind, and the temperature drops with altitude. I took the lead as we turned left at the only intersection on the entire course and plodded upward toward the summit.

"Do you remember my saying that if I really pay attention, I can actually feel the hardening of my heart whenever I get angry?"

"Yes, I do," Marc replied. "You said it was a signal that you were being defensive and withdrawing. A duck-for-cover maneuver, a kind of internal Muhammad Ali rope-a-dope strategy. I think you called it a 'calcification.'"

"That's right. For several months I've been trying to pay attention to that feeling, and I've realized that it comes up in all kinds of different situations—at home, at work, and when I'm sitting in traffic. And every time it comes, if I can manage to fix my attention on it and study it before I react, it doesn't have as much of a hold on me. Most of the time, it doesn't turn into an impulse to act out."

"Interesting," Marc said. "But why do you think that's important?"

"About a month ago, Chris and I had one of those I'm-frustrated-and-need-to-vent-to-someone discussion-slash-arguments. There I was, in the middle of this charged situation, trying to hear what Chris is saying, and at the same time I'm trying to pay attention to the rising sensation of cal-cification in my heart. And here's the really important part. Every single time, without fail, that I latched onto something

Chris said, and my attention wandered away from what was happening in my chest, I got swept up into the argument. And every time, Chris knew it and called me on it. Without fail. She may not have consciously known that I had stopped paying attention and that I had started reacting, but she felt it. She'd say something like, 'You're not being very support-ive,' or 'You're not listening.' And here's the thing. At that moment, she was right. Every time she said it, it reminded me to look back at my heart, and there it was, that sensation of hardening. I think she's the perfect mirror for me."

We were climbing a steep, exposed ridge that passed the Juniper Campground. A giant bay laurel, fully fifteen feet around the trunk, guarded the campground entrance. I felt wonderful, expansive, and I continued talking despite my labored breathing.

"So here I am, smack in the middle of the argument, alter-nately open and caring when I manage to pay attention, and shrinking and defensive when the discussion carries my attention away. I can see the whole thing now, as if it's unfolding before me. It was like I was dancing in a strobe, alternately filled with light and space and flailing in the dark. Each time it got dark, something would poke at me, remind-ing me to turn on the light. I was sitting in the vortex of a very serious moment, and feeling amazement and laughter and sadness all at once.

"The experience verified something I had suspected for a

long time—that there's a faculty that understands when I'm open and receptive, and when I'm not. And it's unerring. It seems all I need to do is cultivate a relationship with that part of myself—nurture it, water it, and let it grow—and it will guide me to the right behavior. The experience was kind of funny, because I was trying to pay attention and repeatedly drifting away, like a narcoleptic president nodding off during the delivery of the State of the Union.

"And it was also sad, because I wasn't sufficiently skilled to maintain full attention. Not having enough of that skill is a kind of a hell, really, because it's essential for finding our way in our business dealings, and our relationships with family, friends, neighbors, and ourselves."

"What did it tell you about you and Chris?" Marc asked. We had just passed Devil's Elbow, and the road began to wind around to the opposite side of the mountain. With three-quarters of a mile of relatively flat road before us, the only real challenge remaining was the final two hundred yards to the summit, the steepest pitch of the climb.

"I'll have to digress to answer that. We've had a very windy summer, and for months I've been staring out of my office window at the branches swaying and the leaves shimmering. I got to thinking about the wind. I couldn't see or feel or hear it through the glass, yet I knew it was there because of the trees. And I realized an interesting thing—that wind is really both air and tree, not just moving air. They aren't really separate, like we usually think of them.

"I also noticed that the branches and leaves only push back against the wind in proportion to how much the wind pushes against them. When Chris and I were arguing, we exchanged energy, like the wind and the trees. But it was our attention that acted as a gauge to tell us if the energy was positive or negative. When it was negative, Chris pushed back, like the branches of the trees. I guess you could say that Chris and I weren't separate during that argument. What emerges is that we're connected in more intimate ways than we commonly imagine. Once we begin to understand this in our most loving relationships, we can begin to see it in all our other relationships. But the part about our not being separate is just an inkling of a realization within me, a possibility that I can just see dimly through the fog, for the first time. It isn't a firm or permanent awareness yet."

I paused to collect my thoughts and then continued. "There's something more. We are connected in more intimate ways than we imagine, but we are also more than just trees buffeted by the random forces of life."

"Go on," Marc replied.

"There was a moment in our quarrel when I was completely drawn in, and both of us were marshaling our defenses around us, preparing to do battle. Things were about to get ugly. And then Chris said to me, 'Dean, Zach's skin has been really bad, we've been awake several nights in a row, and I think we're both very stressed and very tired.' Such grace. Her simple words opened up a space for love to enter, lowering my defenses, pulling us together. I looked into her face and I realized how much I love her." I paused again listening to the wind whispering against the upper reaches of the mountain, feeling a peaceful stillness inside.

"You know," I said, "I can still hear the quiet echo of that moment. How can I look at Chris struggling, just as I struggle, to find inner presence and freedom in the midst of the big forces in life, and not love her? I can't. I can only love and admire her because she's willing to struggle. It's my job to serve her in that struggle, just as she serves me. This is our work together as a loving couple. I saw it so clearly that night. And now I am more aware of this theme always playing in the background. We are here to help each other love more." I smiled, remembering Grandma's admonition.

"Well, we made it," Marc said.

Without my realizing it, we had reached the summit.

Marc said, "Except for the summit of Mount Kilimanjaro in Tanzania, you can see more land surface from the top of Mount Diablo than anywhere else in the world."

I looked out toward the skyline of San Francisco, thirty miles to the west, and then twenty miles past the city to the Farallon Islands, in the hazy northwest. Turning east, I could see the great spine of the Sierra Nevada, where I could pick out Half Dome in Yosemite Valley, and Mount Whitney on the far southeast horizon. I breathed deeply, taking mental pictures. The temperature had dropped to the high thirties, and I was wearing only a sweaty T-shirt and shorts. Gooseflesh rose on my arms and legs. A warm van was waiting to shuttle us back down the mountain.

"There are so many mountains to run up." I said, allowing my gaze to wander over the richly fertile Central Valley on the other side of the mountain from where I live, a valley where half of the country's fruits, nuts, and vegetables are grown.

"Is that a problem?" Marc said.

"Marc, when I'm at my best, I love the notion of an open challenge. Every mountain teaches us something we need to know. When I'm not at my best, I find the whole thing overwhelming."

"So where do you go now?" Marc said.

"Back down the mountain," I joked, knowing it wasn't what Marc meant, but enjoying the wordplay. "It's cold up here, but there's something I have to do first. It's almost the new millennium, and I have a wish for the people of Earth, for the next thousand years." I climbed up to the highest rock and spread my arms wide and yelled: "Fight the postmodern experience!" Then, more softly, so that nobody could hear, I said, "May we all find a deep, profound, and unshakable peace in our own individual hearts. Everything else will take care of itself." As I said it, I visualized the wind picking up my little wish and spreading it to the four corners of the globe. I hoped it would help.

Marc laughed. "Remind them to pay attention and live life directly," he added, obviously recalling our conversation of more than two years ago. So I did, shouting into the wind like a madman.

Sitting in the back of the van, I turned to Marc. "I have a crazy notion that I need to share this idea—that you can feel it whenever you're opening up or closing down. It's a sensation we've all felt, probably thousands and thousands of times, yet we never pay attention to it. I think that if we did so, our relationships would improve. Maybe we could learn together, as a society, and get over some of the big problems we're facing."

"Are you saying that love is good for business?" Marc's eyes twinkled.

Marc continually surprises me. Knowing his atheistic tendencies, I hadn't ventured to call the thing that my heart was opening to "love," at least not outside the context of marriage. Yet Marc had immediately defined it as I had. And he hadn't stopped there—he had extrapolated further, pointing out possible implications for the business world, even as I'd been on the point of doing.

"Yes and no," I said. "Yes, opening the heart to love is good for business—if you believe that forming relationships is good for business. But no, opening to love isn't good for business, if you mean immediate benefits for the bottom line. Sometimes the best, most loving action in a business relationship is to walk away from a deal and say no. It depends on the circumstances. Unfortunately, walking away from a business deal in an open, caring way demands that we keep the long-term perspective in mind. Many businesspeople won't have the patience for that, or the tolerance."

"Be careful with that message," Marc said, looking more serious. "People won't want to listen to the second part of what you're saying. The skills that are required in order to succeed in the outer, material world aren't the same as those required for succeeding in the inner world. People will try to manipulate what you're saying for their personal gain and profit. They'll convince themselves they're open to a situation when they're really not."

"I know," I said, feeling the sorrow in my voice. "But here's something I also know. It can't be faked. We're either truly opening to love, or we aren't, and we're either truly paying attention to it, or we're not. It can't be managed, or scheduled. It may not change anything in the outer world that we can see right away, but at some deep, hidden level, everybody will understand if it's present or not."

Marc leaned back and smiled. The other runners in the van had stopped talking. For several minutes they had listened to our conversation. We sat in silence for a while. Finally, Marc said, "Most people will be in too much of a hurry to try to find this."

"I'm a little frightened, Marc. It scares me to think I'm considering trying to write this idea down. I'm not very skilled at paying attention. I fail all the time, and it'll be easy to find fault with the messenger. I have so much to learn. I can sense inside myself many unexplored cold, dark granite surfaces, and who knows what lies beyond them. If Chris is right, as she usually is, my next lesson lies in the area of judgment. But who knows? I do know this much: ever since that rainy night two years ago, when I recognized my own desperation and determined to address it head-on, my life has had more meaning and purpose. The lessons continue to unfold, and my understanding continues to deepen. The funny thing is, nothing has changed at all. I'm married to the same person. I live in the same house. I work at the same job. But my relationship to it all is different, more full and satisfying. As long as I'm following this path, I'm no longer so desperate. Who knows where it will lead?"

We had arrived at the school parking lot. We'd come all the way back to where we'd started, back to our everyday lives. "Who would want to know?" Marc asked. Pausing for a moment, he turned toward me. "Are we running Wednesday night?"

"I wouldn't miss it for anything."

Marc then turned to Joe, our dear friend and driver. "Thanks," he said. "You know we couldn't do this without you."

That afternoon, I sat on the sofa while Zach played with his wooden trains, and I wrote a letter to him.

Dear Zach,

I've been thinking about what I would do if I knew I only had one day left to live. So, because I don't really know if I do, I wanted to write you a letter about it.

What would I do if I knew I only had one day left to live? I would start by going for a run. During that run I would smell each smell, the roses and the horse droppings, with equal joy. I would listen to the leaves rustling in the trees, and I would watch the red-winged blackbirds against bright yellow mustard flower with a sense of awe and wonder. I would run up the Mauler one last time. And I would thank it for remaining such a consistent challenge over the years.

I would skip work and spend the day with you and Mom, playing in the sandbox, making holes by pushing sticks in, feeling the sand pushing back, admiring your intensity about the importance of this activity. And after you went to bed, I would thank Mom for making me want to be a better person. I would tell her how much I appreciate the way she calls ahead to the preschool to find out what they are serving for snack time, so she can make something for you that looks just like it. I would listen intently as we reminisced about all the wonderful experiences we shared. And then, we would make love one last time, and then I would scratch her head until I heard the soft rhythm of her sleep breathing. And after listening to that sweet music for a while, I would sit down to write you a letter trying to give you the best advice I have, which would be something like this:

Enlightenment was never my personal experience. In fact, my life was quite ordinary. I gratefully accept this and would not trade my experience for anyone else's. I did learn some valuable things along the way that I found useful, so I want to pass them on to you in the form of advice.

First, as Socrates suggested when he said "The unexamined life is not worth living," let self-study and a spirit of inquiry become a way of life for you. Use extreme honesty and diligence in this endeavor. Get to know exactly what both the opening and the closing of your heart feels like. Learn its temperature, its pulse, and its texture. If you do, you will learn about the freedom to act out of love, rather than reacting as a victim of your own fears.

Engage in a pointless activity like running that brings you peace of mind. Make this activity a regular part of your day. Stick with this activity when you love doing it and when you hate doing it. It will teach you that everything has its seasons, including your own physical body, your own thoughts, your own feelings, and the world around you. And over time, you will learn that there is a place within yourself that is calm and peaceful despite the changing patterns. And eventually you will learn to discriminate between the real problems of life and the self-inflicted ones.

This is not to say that you can somehow bypass the struggles and troubles of life. There are real problems that cannot be avoided or ignored. You need to look no farther than your own itchy skin to know the truth of this. Pain and sorrow are a genuine part of life, but they are not to be pushed away. They too are to be studied and embraced. They will teach you compassion for yourself and for others. It is this compassion that will connect you to the community of humankind.

Even the intense, but more synthetic emotions of anger or frustration can be great teachers. Use them as reminders to pay attention to your intentions. If you do this, you will learn that the real miracle in life is that just by examining your own motives and agenda without trying to interfere, your own words and deeds will change to more harmonious actions all by themselves. Just the act of examination causes these intense feelings of anger and frustration to lose some of their grip over us. Without doing anything except paying attention to them. Anger and frustration will visit you many thousands of times in your life, but you will never cease to be amazed by the transformative power of attention. It is life's miracle.

And finally, go easy on yourself and others. To be human is to be imperfect. To be an authentic human is to learn from the imperfections. And don't forget to laugh. We live at the contradictory intersections of the spiritual and the material worlds, at the strange crossroads of attention and distraction, and, quite often, it is a funny place to be. Tell people you love that you love them. It feels good to say it, and it is always nice to hear.

Know in your heart forever that I love you very very much.

Love,
Dad

Even as I signed my name, I knew I was issuing Zach a lifelong challenge. I don't know when he will be old enough to make the choice to establish the inner search as his primary motivation, or even if he ever will. What I do know is, if he does, he will likely do so in a world that generally doesn't value or understand such an undertaking. And he will struggle—just as everyone who consciously takes up the search does. And yet, I also know I can't advise him to live in any other way.

19

Running With Justin

"Someday, after we have mastered
the winds, the waves, the tide
and gravity, we shall harness for God
the energies of love.
Then, for the second time in the history
Of the world, man will have discovered fire."
—Pierre Teilhard de Chardin

It's no secret among those I work with that I graduated from Kellogg Graduate School of Management, and that I conduct admissions interviews for the program. In an average year, one or two people will approach me for advice about getting into a top business school, or they'll ask me for a letter of recommendation. This year, it was Justin's turn.

Justin is one of those amazing young professionals who seem to have everything going for them—technical expertise, strong communication skills, business acumen, and solid interpersonal skills. He represents the hope of our future.

From the first time we met, when he came to work for me, I had him pegged as a star. But if Justin has one shortcoming, it's a tendency to think too much like an engineer, approaching life as if it can be managed.

I wasn't surprised when Justin asked me for advice about getting into business school. Later, when he was in town for a meeting, he asked if we could go running together. Always happy to oblige such a request, I met Justin at the Embassy Suites, and we set out on a flat, six-mile loop that wound through tree-lined residential streets and bike trails.

I had a hidden agenda for the run. Justin had confided to me that he had attended a Harvard Business School open house, and that the recruiter had told him that Harvard was seeking applicants who, fifteen years after graduation, would appear on the front page of the *Wall Street Journal* with "HBS" after their names. Justin had stars in his eyes, and I felt it was my duty to confront him about his motivations for applying to business school in the first place.

Each of the top business schools has a unique personality. I had always considered Kellogg and Stanford as the most collegial schools, and I'd thought of Chicago, MIT, Wharton, and Harvard as having a more competitive, quantitative atmosphere. Always curious about the competition, I said, "So what's the main essay question for Stanford this year?" We had settled into a pleasant rhythm and were headed south on Civic Drive, before turning onto a paved bicycle trail.

"It's 'What matters most to you, and why?'"

I couldn't believe my good fortune. The question expressed exactly what I thought Justin needed to consider regarding his business school aspirations. "That's a great question. It gives me hope for the top-flight business schools. What *does* matter most to you, and why?"

"Well," Justin said, "I have five things I want to make sure the admissions committee knows about me, and I think I can work them all into the answer."

"Justin, come on! Not you, too!" I pleaded. "I'm going to give you the same advice I give every business school candidate. Don't try to answer the questions by saying what you think the admissions people want to hear. They've heard it all before, and they have a very good BS detector—they can easily tell a genuine answer from a fake one. Don't assume you know what they're looking for, because what they're looking for is real people with the courage to tell them exactly what's important to them. Besides, even if you don't get into business school, it's an important question to ask yourself, don't you think? We shouldn't go through life without knowing what's most important to us, should we? Otherwise we're doomed to live somebody else's vision of what's important."

Justin was quiet for a long time. I had always been a supportive fan, and I could tell that my challenge had caught him off guard. I waited while we ran on the bike trail, passing the Heather Farms pool where I had met Chris when we were on the master's team, in January, 1983. Chris had been an Olympic-caliber swimmer in her youth, and was a master's record holder when we met. At the time, I was an out-of-shape, five-years-retired, three-one-hundredths-of-a-second shy of high school All-America swimmer. Yet somehow, despite competing in the pool, we fell in love. A little more than two and a half years later, we married in the Garden Center, which I could see now over my right shoulder, and which overlooked the swim lanes where Chris and I had fallen in love. Chris had said it must be true love if I could love her in swimming cap and goggles. I smiled at the sweet memory of taking our vows while we watched people jump off the high dive, Chris's bouquet trembling in time with our nerves.

Finally, Justin spoke. "Dean, why did you go to business school?"

"Insecurities."

"What?"

"My junior year at UCLA was my defining year in college. I lived in a two-bedroom apartment in Westwood with my best friend from high school, Bob, and two other guys I admired very much. Now, you've got to understand. I never studied at UCLA. Instead, I drank a lot of coffee the night before exams and rifled through the entire book in one sitting, and that's about it. One of my roommates, whom we called Bobcat to avoid confusing him with the other Bob, was working his butt off to get into medical school. Bobcat would come up to me and say, 'Dean, we're not smart like Bob and Steve.' At the same time, Steve, whom we all thought was brilliant, would come up to me and say, 'Dean we just don't work hard like the Bobs do.'

"Well, it didn't take me very long to put that little Mendel's square together and figure out that I was the lazy, stupid one. And for some ridiculous reason, that conclusion stuck with me. Nine years later, I looked up from my middle-management job at Chevron to see Bobcat working as a doctor and the other Bob one step away from making partner at a Big Six consulting firm, and Steve getting close to the top of a medium-sized recruiting company. Their careers seemed much more vital than mine, and I just had to figure out if I was really the lazy, stupid one. So I applied to five top-ranking business schools, and I got rejected by all of them. Every single one."

"So then what did you do?" Justin asked.

"I went backpacking alone that summer, so that I could have some quiet time to think about what I wanted to do. After staring into a week's worth of campfires and watching sparks rise into the night sky, I realized that I had sent in applications that catered to what I thought the schools wanted to hear, and that gave no sense of who I really was. I decided to give business school another shot.

"The next year, I applied to the number-one-ranked

business school in the country, and I was fortunate to get in, but it was on my own terms, because I had told the admissions committee exactly what I thought. I had answered the 'What do you want to do when you grow up?' question with the truth—I had no idea, but I hoped that business school would help me explore some options.

"While most of my classmates treated the B-school experience as a two-year job interview, I had some demons to slay. I worked hard at my studies to prove that I could, but the point is, it wasn't until I answered the admissions questions with a sense of who I really was that I got in. I was even accepted by a couple of the same schools that had rejected my application the previous year."

Justin was quiet again. I knew my answer had been a little more revealing than he had expected. Finally, he turned and said, "What did you learn from B-school?"

"I learned a lot of things. First, I learned that it's a lot of fun to hang out with a bunch of bright, energetic people, because they bring out the best in you. So before you decide to attend one of these schools, take a good look at the student body, because you'll be spending a lot of time with those people. It turned out that I learned more from the other students than I did from the professors."

We had turned off the bicycle trail and were passing De La Salle High School, whose football team held the longest high school winning streak in the country, ninety-four straight games. As we ran past, the sound of boys grunting and slapping pads reached us as waves of players crashed into blocking sleds. We turned west and headed into the neighborhoods. As we wound around a blind hairpin curve, we squeezed to the side of the road just as a car sped by without seeing us.

I continued, "I also liked learning about statistics—trends, variations, probabilities."

"Why?" Justin said.

"When I looked at statistics, I saw in a very visual way how, even in a tightly controlled process, no two screws ever come off an assembly line with exactly the same thread measurements. Nature just cannot be pinned down sufficiently to allow the production of two screws that are exactly alike. To someone like me, who views everything as a process, the wonderful mathematics of statistics changes how we interpret the events and happenings in our own lives. It's a mathematics that teaches you to expect variation as a normal part of life."

"What do you mean?"

"For example, Chris and I could be getting along wonderfully for months on end. Then, all of a sudden, for no apparent reason, we could have a terrible day of unrelenting arguments. We're having a statistical 'outlier' kind of day. It doesn't mean that our marriage has soured. It means that our marriage follows the same behavior that all processes follow. Some things just can't be explained—and that's normal. The more you look for this, the more you see it everywhere. And as you watch it happening over and over, you realize there are no guaranteed outcomes in life. The best you can do is put a probabilistic mask into place. And once you realize that, you can cut yourself and everyone else some slack. It creates quite a lot of room for forgiveness."

"What do you mean by a 'probabilistic mask'?" Justin said.

"For example, you want to go to business school, because you think others will realize you're serious about your career, and it'll afford you opportunities that will help you make it to the front page of the *Wall Street Journal*. But the *Wall Street Journal* may not happen for you. It's just that the probability is more favorable if you attend business school. But the same principle applies to the everyday process of raising children, for example. Everyone likes to think that if they spend quality time with their kids, they'll grow up to be fine adults. But by all accounts, the parents of at least one of the students who opened fire at Columbine were very active in their son's life. Yet the boy goes on a killing rampage. And all of a sudden, it's not so simple to say that good parenting ensures good children. Yet it's what we try to do, and when things go wrong we're quick to blame the parents.

"Sometimes, it's not the parents' fault. The truth, as far as I can see, is that active, involved parenting only puts the probabilities in place to make a normal, well-adjusted child. I find statistics a much more useful model than breaking things down into black and white, and I find that probabilities model my own experience much better. Thinking statistically shows us that it's good to plan for the future, but it's not wise to get too attached to the anticipated results."

"But some things *are* black and white," Justin protested.

"Not that I can find," I said. "Take car noise, for example. Most people would say it's a black-and-white issue. Is car noise good or bad?"

"Bad," Justin said. "I live near a freeway. It's noisy all the time, and it gets pretty irritating."

"That's exactly how most people feel about car noise. But a few minutes ago, you and I moved out of the way of a speeding car without even seeing it. We knew it was coming around a blind corner because we heard it. Can you imagine what a world of silent cars would be like for runners? There wouldn't be any of us left!" I was teasing, and I felt a little guilty about setting him up.

Justin fell silent again. Only our breathing broke the stillness as we ran. Finally, he spoke, shifting gears now. "Dean, why didn't you take the job with the RadioGear and Sancho alliance? It was a great opportunity, yet you turned it down." Justin was referring to a recently announced alliance between our company, RadioGear, and the world's leading Internet products company, a union calculated to marry the world of wireless communications with the Internet. It promised to be a huge opportunity for those involved, and it clearly foretold the future of both meteoric industries. To the surprise of many and displeasure of some, I had turned down a significant promotion to get in on the ground floor of the new alliance.

It was my turn to be quiet. I wondered if Justin, at his stage of life, would understand. Finally I said, "I just don't want to chase windmills anymore. I turned the job down because, when I searched my heart, I knew, despite all the sound and logical reasons my head was giving me, that it wasn't what I'm supposed to do. There are too many other things that are more important to me right now. I can't see spending my life commuting to Silicon Valley. It's not worth it to me anymore. I can't see myself working the long hours I used to. I no longer have the energy and patience for it. I want more time to spend with Chris and Zach."

"What you're saying is that you want to achieve some balance in your life," Justin said.

"Actually, yes and no. I wouldn't call it achieving balance."

"But I thought that's what you were saying."

"I know, it sounded that way, but what I actually said is that I searched my heart and realized that taking the job wasn't the right thing for me, right now. Don't get me wrong. For most people, I think balance is a good thing that would serve them well. But I think we as a society are very confused about this notion. Everybody says they want balance, but if you look a little deeper, it's their own happiness that they're really trying to manage, and happiness can't be managed, at least not in the way we're used to managing things.

"People think that with a little ingenuity and planning, they can get up in the morning, go for an effortless three-mile jog, arrive at the office for a stimulating, high-powered day of work, then come home and spend some quality time with the kids, and finish off the evening with great sex—and then repeat the process the next day. We all like to think that if we just managed our time a little better, we would find this mythical easy, perpetual happiness. The truth is, if you don't spend time figuring out what's important to you, and why, you'll continue to be tempted to try to squeeze in just a little bit more. And, before you know it, you'll be back wishing you had a forty-eight-hour day.

"MBAs are particularly vulnerable to this, so beware. If we neglect to examine our lives, we can fool ourselves into thinking that we can have an upwardly mobile career and a frictionless family life. We think we can have endless excitement and perfect peace. But very often, these things contradict each other, and we wonder why our actual experiences in life don't match our expectations. I think balance is a probabilistic result, rather than just one more thing to be managed and achieved."

"A probabilistic result of what?" Justin said.

"A probabilistic result of learning to listen to your own

heart. I believe that when people start attending to what their heart is telling them, they begin to find meaning and purpose. Everything else begins to take care of itself, resulting in a natural balance. That's all there is. You can't plan what your heart will tell you, and you can't manage it. Just know what your heart is saying, and that's it. There's nothing else to do. Of course, advice like this drives MBAs crazy."

"But Dean, there are difficulties in life. Are you saying I should just drop everything and travel around the world because my heart says it doesn't want to go to work anymore? What about my responsibilities? Even if I did quit my job, I couldn't afford to travel around the world. And if I keep my job, I don't have time to travel around the world. Everybody is stuck in the trade-off between time and money. Life involves compromise."

I laughed, looking into the face of a more talented but also a little more lost version of myself at Justin's age, telling me about life. Justin had just expressed the same viewpoint I had heard from nearly every motivated professional person I had ever known, yet I also knew it to be a viewpoint that leads to the quiet desperation about which Thoreau wrote. Even the most successful and talented among us are not immune. It was my view at Justin's age, and it's a view I still struggle with, because it's part of our common cultural, upwardly mobile heritage. "Justin, I can't deny that life involves compromises. It's my experience that it does. But I would venture to say that it involves far less compromise than we often lead ourselves to believe."

"What do you mean?"

"I, too, sometimes fantasize about dropping everything and traveling around the world. And, just like you, I have responsibilities. The difference may be that when I look deeply into my heart, the notion of turning my back on my responsibilities doesn't really make my heart sing. I sometimes entertain the thought because it's a pleasurable diversion, but that's all it is. The only important thing about having such thoughts is to be aware that you're having them, and know yourself well enough to understand what those thoughts are really telling you. I usually experience escape fantasies when I'm taking things too seriously. They serve as a signal to let go a little."

"What do you mean, let go?"

"I mean, let go of some of the relentless cultural messages that continually push us into doing things we'd never undertake without those cultural pressures. Let me put it this way. I live a nice, upper-middle-class American life. I enjoy the challenges and even the distractions of work, more than I ever have. But I can't see turning my life over to the work, putting in countless hours just to make more money. What's the point? You could say I'm trying to achieve balance in my life, but it would be more accurate to say that a balanced life is the result of listening to what my heart is telling me. My heart tells me I have enough house, enough income, enough car, enough stuff. I don't want any more.

"When I look at this issue from my heart, there's no compromise, no time-versus-money bind. In my case, I find that
listening to my heart clarifies the situation. I have family and
work, and running and writing. When I actually live this way,
life gets pretty simple, and a twenty-four-hour day is enough.
It's only my head, influenced by the American culture surrounding us, that tells me I'm making a compromise, that I
could be making more money, living in a bigger house,
wielding more power and influence, and getting better forti-
fied for retirement.

"At the same time—and this will sound like a contradiction—I recognize that I am very lucky. I've paid my token to
pass through the suburban turnstile. I live in a nice, clean,
healthy environment with excellent running trails, close to a
vibrant city. I recognize that everyone has standards, but we
never take the time to ask ourselves what they are. If we did,
we would be asking ourselves a whole lot more questions
about why we sacrifice so much of our lives to obtain more of
what we don't need."

Justin's tone became serious and slightly confrontational.
"There are people in the world who work long hours, start
new businesses, and run big companies, but they don't do it
just for selfish reasons. They create jobs and develop new
industries for people just like you to work in, and these are
good things. Their efforts promote the economy, and this is

good for everybody. Are you saying they should follow their hearts instead of working hard for the common good?"

"Don't get me wrong!" I said. "Hard work and innovation are important, for sure. People need work, and a good economy takes care of many real problems. We all benefit from innovation—for one thing, I would much rather have a toothache today than at any other time in history. I also believe that there are people who, if they listened to their hearts, would still be compelled to work hard and create jobs and innovations for the rest of us. I have no doubt that Big Jack is one of those people. It's what Big Jack was born to do. But I also believe that most of us aren't built to work all the time. People see the glamour of Big Jack's lifestyle—the travel, the big meetings, the important decisions—and they think they want that, too. But very few of us ever stop to think of the sacrifices that lifestyle entails. Big Jack is a good man, and I'm sure he's a good father, but I wonder if he ever questions himself about the amount of time he spent with his kids."

"Are you saying you can't be a high-level executive or start a new business, and be an involved father, too?" Justin challenged.

"I'm saying I'm not sure that our culture guides us properly in this area. I can't prove it, but I believe there's a force guiding us in the universe, and that if we knew how to follow that force, we'd do an even better job of raising our children and providing for the common good. I also believe that a part of us is attuned to that force all the time, and that in our hearts, we know when we're opening to this force and when we're shutting it out. It's our job to understand our own heart and follow what it's telling us.

"What I can say from my own, personal, direct experience is that I'm better off when I pay attention to what my heart tells me. And—who knows—maybe your heart is telling you to go to Harvard and start a dotcom, work lots of hours, and make the front page of *The Wall Street Journal* in fifteen years' time. I can't say. You can only know from within yourself if you're being guided that way. Right now, I know I'm not."

"You can't be saying that we should let our economy be driven by a feeling in our hearts," Justin said, incredulous, and then added, "That's an awfully subjective thing to base our livelihoods on. It just isn't rational."

"Justin," I said, "life is not a rational process. If it were, the engineers would be the happiest people among us, and we know that isn't true." I winked at Justin, an engineer by training. He appeared to be taking the teasing well. I went on, "I have to ask why it's ridiculous to suggest that we should pay closer attention to what our hearts are telling us. It's no more ridiculous than what's driving the economy now."

"What do you mean? Hard work and innovation drive the economy now, and it works quite well," Justin said.

I paused for a moment, my stride flowing with renewed

energy. I had no idea from what recesses of my mind the words were forming themselves, but before I continued, I checked my intentions. We were both learning something here, although in my case I still didn't know what, so I just let the words flow. As I spoke, I listened with as much interest as Justin: "Let me put it this way. Two hundred and fifty years ago, Adam Smith developed the notion of an invisible hand guiding the economy. He basically said that impersonal market forces automatically direct resources to their highest and best use. In other words, a rare and precious metal like gold automatically goes into the making of wedding rings, because it symbolizes something that is rare and precious in our lives. By the same token, we will never see a television set made out of gold, because there are too many other, less expensive and equally functional materials that we can use to build one. If we did see a gold TV, we would question the sanity of the person who'd felt impelled to create such an outrageous, ostentatious display. The notion of an invisible hand is so universally accepted that it's become unquestioned MBA dogma."

So that's where this is leading, I thought. It was a very old question, left over from my undergraduate days as an economics major at UCLA. Even at the time, I had sensed a basic oversight in Adam Smith's theories, but I couldn't put my finger on it. Adam Smith had understood that the process that flows best is the one with the fewest encumbrances.

Adam Smith remained silent about the flow of inputs into the process. This was the area that needed further examination.

"You're talking about capitalism," Justin said. "Surely you aren't saying you're against capitalism, are you?"

"On the contrary, I'm a great believer in capitalism. I can't think of a better organizing principle. I've been to communist countries, and I've seen firsthand how that system doesn't work. The engine of capitalism has brought us a golden age of material wealth. I'm saying that we in the business profession like to think of ourselves as practical people who get things done, unencumbered by light-headed and arbitrary ideas like listening to our hearts. There are other, separate specialties such as religion that cover that ground. But when you come right down to it, businesspeople will swear up and down that an invisible hand is guiding the economy. We know that businesspeople don't object to the notion of an invisible force. So I have to ask, what is it exactly that businesspeople object to? The invisible hand is just the sum total of our individual motivations.

"You and I come from a Malcolm Baldridge Quality Award company. It's very clear to us that one of the first things you examine when you try to raise quality in a process is the input. Well, the economy is just another process. Perhaps, as a culture, we can improve the quality of what we're producing by more closely inspecting the real input into the economy: our motivations."

"I thought you just said we're living in a golden age. Now you're saying our economy produces poor quality. Aren't you contradicting yourself?"

It was a good question. "I'm saying that capitalism as it stands isn't the full answer. Have you ever wondered why business executives make so much more money than school teachers? I mean, can we honestly say that cranking out an advertising campaign designed to convince people to choose one toothpaste over another is a higher and better use of talent than educating our children? I'm not sure I'm ready to make that claim. Look at it this way. The last 250 years have been about developing science and opening the marketplace. Perhaps the next 250 years will be about better understanding the motivations behind our advancements. Who knows where that would lead us? But I would venture to say this much. I think it's a place where I'd like to live.

"Here's an idea that might make it more palatable. Maybe we should give it a business buzzword. Call it 'examining the economic right force.' Then, instead of asking if we're listening to our hearts, we could ask if we're 'examining the economic right force' within us. We might feel better about it." I could sense that I'd pushed too hard, too fast. Justin just didn't want to hear this.

"I've got to walk for a minute," Justin said. We slowed while Justin collected his thoughts. "What businesspeople object to," he said firmly, "is the notion of having to defend themselves for loving their work, starting new businesses, and maybe even getting wealthy in the process. Everybody assumes bad intentions on the part of businesspeople. Who are you to decide if a businessperson's intentions are good or bad?"

"Justin, I agree. I'm walking on some pretty speculative terrain here. I'm not saying that anybody should set themselves up to judge whether other people's intentions are good or bad. It's a personal act. All I'm saying is that our intentions should be examined and understood as clearly as possible. We should pay attention to them, and that's all. I believe that if we pay attention to our intentions, the rest will naturally begin to take care of itself. I'd be a man of very little faith if I thought that interference was required. Perhaps we need a business school class that teaches us how to begin to systematically explore our intentions."

Again Justin was quiet. I enjoyed the walking. Overhead, the reds and yellows of fall burned brightly, reminding me of growing up in Michigan and going to the Franklin cider mill for fresh warm doughnuts in a greasy brown bag, washed down with cool apple juice.

"I don't understand."

"Let me put it this way. You're about to enjoy the great privilege of attending a big-time business school. But with privilege comes responsibility. When you graduate, you'll be managing some pretty big forces in life, and the livelihoods of lots of people will depend on you. All I'm saying is that you should try to figure out exactly what your personal agenda is in all this, and once you know that, the rest will begin to take care of itself. There's nothing to manage here. If you don't do this self-examination, you'll be much more prone to fall victim to the herd mentality that prevails in business school."

"Herd mentality?"

"Yes. I attended business school with some of the brightest, most energetic, and nicest people I could ever hope to meet. All of them had been enormously successful prior to business school, and the promise of the future looked even better. As students, we learned all about the tools and techniques for managing and manipulating a business. But we never once stopped to ask ourselves why we were attending business school in the first place. I think we all would have been surprised by the real answers. Anyway, when it came time to go to job interviews, almost everybody suddenly wanted to become a consultant, just because that's what everybody else wanted. Especially me. I interviewed with all the big-name consulting firms and even managed to snag a couple of job offers. In the end, I didn't go. The funny thing is, two years after graduation, almost everybody I knew who'd gone into consulting had quit. They were burned out. The money and prestige ended up meaning not nearly as much as it had when we were competing for interviews. Funny. I now consider it my sworn duty to make all consultants question the meaning of their lives."

Now it was Justin's turn to surprise me. "All you've done is push the invisible hand back a little farther. You say we need to examine our own intentions in business. Then you say that the rest will take care of itself. Aren't you just moving the invisible hand back a little farther? What have we gained?"

Now it was my turn to be quiet. We continued walking, and as we did, I ruffled fallen oak leaves with my feet, the way Zach does when he walks on a trail. I could see now why he did it—it's fun. Justin was right. All I had done was substitute the notion that the heart's natural desire to move toward love should drive the economy, instead of leaving things up to the often unexamined impulses that comprise the invisible hand. Both forces are equally mysterious and invisible to the untrained eye.

After a while, I spoke: "I know what you're saying, and you're right. All I can say is, we could all use a little systematic exploring of our hearts. And if we did that, I suspect that quite a number of unnecessary problems would begin to sort themselves out. But nothing in our culture prepares us to pay attention to our intentions. Even worse, nothing prepares us to examine something and then not do anything about it. I'm fully ready to admit that I could be wrong about everything I've said today. I reserve the right to keep pursuing my investigations, but so far, it hasn't been my experience that I'm way off base about any of this. I can only fall back on what a great teacher once said to me: 'Go see for yourself.' I've suggested nothing radical or harmful, and as far as I know, nobody has died by trying to pay more attention to his heart, by listening to what's happening inside before acting in the outside world. It won't hurt you or anybody else. You can do it during the normal course of your life. You just might discover something useful."

We had emerged from the neighborhood, a few blocks from the hotel. Justin said, "Dean, how do I go about doing this?"

"Well, you like to run. A very practical place to start would be to go for a run all by yourself every day, with no company, no headphones, and no distractions. When you're out there, ask yourself this question: What's most important to me, and why? When you get home, write down what came to you. Do this repeatedly. Try not to succumb to early-deadline pressure to get your application in, and don't fall too much in love with your first answer. Keep asking the question. See what you learn in the process. You might be very surprised by what you find. Things are never quite as they seem at first, at least not for me."

20

The Runner and the Path

"The sky was still blue, the sun still beaming when they locked me up. But during my incarceration it had begun to rain. The legendary Seattle rain. It was a thin gray rain; hard and fast and cold. In it, we had to walk four blocks from the Public Safety Building to the Zillers' Jeep—we were at its mercy. As was my custom in such elements I hunkered against the rain, drew my head into my collar, turned my eyes to the street, tensed my footsteps and proceeded in misery. But my hosts, I soon noticed, reacted in quite another way. They strolled calmly and smoothly, their bodies perfectly relaxed. They did not hunch away from the rain but rather glided through it. They directed their faces to it and did not flinch as it drummed their cheeks. They almost reveled in it. Somehow, I found this significant. The Zillers accepted the rain. They were not at odds with it, they did not deny it or combat it; they accepted it and went with it in harmony and ease. I tried it myself. I relaxed my neck and shoulders and turned my gaze into the wet. I let it do to me what it would. Of course, it was not trying to do anything to me. What a silly notion. It was simply falling as rain should, and I a man, another phenomenon of nature, was sharing the space in which it fell. It was much better regarding it that way. I got no wetter than I would

have otherwise, and if I did not actually enjoy the wetting, at least I was free of my tension. I could even smile. What I smiled at was the realization that I had been in the Zillers' company less than fifteen minutes and already their example had altered my behavior. Surely, I was on the right track."
  —Tom Robbins, *Another Roadside Attraction*

T he red numbers glowed through the darkness: 2:58 A.M. Outside, a rare Northern California fall thunderstorm gathered in the distance, the remnant of a tropical storm from the south. Bright flashes broke the night, illuminating trees like glowing skeletons. But that isn't what woke me up.

The previous morning, a press release had announced that SkyReach would merge with Mobile East Telephone, and that Mobile East would have controlling interest in the new joint venture. It had also been announced that the joint venture would be headquartered in New Jersey. It meant that the Walnut Creek office of SkyReach, my customer, would be closed. And it meant that my job was going away, only in my case I didn't have stock options and a golden parachute to fall back on.

I knew I wouldn't be able to get back to sleep, and I decided not to fight it. In the darkness, I pulled on a pair of running shorts and slipped out the door. The sultry night air matched my anxiety. It's one thing to conclude that I don't identify myself with my job while I've still got it, but quite another to maintain that detachment when my job is going away.

I started up the hill through the tunnel of trees that lined the next block. When I emerged, swiftly moving silver-black clouds covered and released the moon. Behind these early storm troopers, a flotilla of menacing battleships lumbered forward, shooting lightning bolts at the ground. It was easy to imagine myself as their quarry. I found my rhythm just as the wind picked up. I had no idea how far or how long I'd run. I decided to make loops through the neighborhood and stay near home. The low rumbling in the distance moved steadily closer as a second storm gathered force in my head.

What will happen to me? What will I do about Zach's medical care? How will I find another job where I'll make as much money? What skills have I got? I don't want to look for a job now, and I don't like the interview process. I hate starting new jobs. A few loose sprinkles struck my face and neck.

The first time I had looked for a job, in 1982, the last serious recession was rolling across the country. I was eager to work, just out of college and ready to begin my "real" life. I thought I had good qualities—sincerity, a strong desire to make things better in the world. Still, I couldn't find work. I applied to 122 companies and got three responses. The business world of the early 1980s placed little value on idealism such as mine. Looking for work was a hard, soul-searching process that engendered self-doubts. I didn't want to go through it all over again. In 1982, I had just withdrawn my last hundred dollars from the bank when I finally received an offer. That was about as close as I ever wanted to cut it.

I tried talking myself out of my fears. *The economy's better than it's ever been. We have no debts other than the mortgage. We have a good amount of savings. I went to graduate school to gain marketable skills. I'm just imagining things. A new job will be easy to find.* But it didn't work. Each argument spun off counterarguments and fresh doubts. All the fears I had spent my professional life trying to manage and contain popped out of my subconscious and showed their ugly heads. Boiled down, they expressed my deep concerns about worthiness and acceptance.

Outside, the wind swirled in all directions. Inside, my thoughts spiraled downward toward the abyss. Above me, the trees groaned as the wind pushed them about. I ran and ran into the night. I looked up just as a last, lone star was swallowed by the clouds. I would see no more stars tonight. I wanted to turn back, but I couldn't. Restlessness awaited me in bed. There had to be something more. The rain picked up.

Continuing to run, I looked deep into my fears, until finally I let them wash over me. If I was going to be afraid, I might as well be really afraid. I gave up, surrendering to the storm, the night, the merger, the thoughts, the fears. They were all true, because they were all present. I wouldn't fight them. My

T-shirt was soaked through.

I came to a small neighborhood park, edged with trees that gave way to a grassy clearing. During the day, children played catch here, while rollerbladers practiced their tricky moves. Now the park was empty. For unfathomable reasons, I stopped and, for an instant, the wind paused. In the briefest moment of silence and calm, from the bushes I heard a throaty, chuffing noise. *Coyotes?* I looked more deeply, and a flash of lightning illuminated a family of deer—father, mother, and baby, huddling in the rain, staring out at me. The buck and I locked each other's eyes for the duration of the flash. *How difficult it must be to live in the open without shelter,* I thought. *Will I wind up like that deer?* Just as a runner realizes that the pain in a knee can be traced to a worn-out pair of shoes, I realized in that moment that my fears weren't what I thought them to be.

They were all still true. I was still concerned about Zach's health care. I was still anxious about starting a new job. I still wanted to provide for my family. But what I was really afraid of was being trapped in the same corporate experience all over again. In that moment, I knew I had learned what I needed to know about that kind of experience, at least for now. Perhaps I would need to come back to it later, but for now I had wrung all the lessons of relationships and the heart that I could from this job. It was time to move on. I had lingered in my role because it paid well. It was convenient. I had grown comfortable, but for almost a year, I had felt that it was time to move on. Now the universe seemed to be saying, "If you won't do it, I'll close the shop and move you." I found comfort in that realization, though I didn't understand why. It was just time for a new experience, that's all.

Yet it made no logical sense. None of my anxieties suddenly disappeared. I still had to find a job. I still had to provide for my family. But I wasn't like the deer. I knew that people would ask what I planned to do, and that I'd have to say I had no idea. I would be able to say only that it would be a different experience, and I knew this would puzzle them. But for tonight, I could live with it, and I'd be able to sleep again.

As I turned homeward, I thought of a story that Marc had told, months ago. He said, "When I sign up to do an Ironman, I like the fear of not knowing. I like not knowing if I've trained well enough to finish. I like not knowing if my bicycle will break down. It's the not knowing that makes it interesting. Who would want to know? Life is like that. I'm in my midfifties, and when I look back, I realize that despite all the doubts and the not knowing, things work out. My friends who left their corporate jobs to start businesses were terrified, but now they all agree it was the best decision they ever made. It kind of makes you wonder why you ever worried in the first place."

The rain picked up, and I ran faster. I visualized the legendary October dawn on the Kona coast. I was at the start of the Hawaiian Ironman, treading water and waiting for the starter's cannon, not knowing . . .

An old business adage rang in my head: "The only constant is change." I had considered it to be just another bland management platitude, designed to rationalize a new organizational chart, usually with the name of the person imparting that clichéd wisdom on the topmost rung. But on a deep cellular level, I felt the genuine wisdom behind the words. Roles change. Jobs are born and die. Thoughts change. Emotions change. My body changes. Even how I look at these things changes. Nothing is permanent or stable. Everything moves. Nothing stays put, yet something unknowable somehow transcends and sees it all.

It's similar to the way there are good runs and bad runs, different trails, changing seasons, yet through it all something laces up its shoes and heads out the door to experience it, all of it. And there in the dark night, I came once again to the question that any self-respecting person engaged in a journey of self-discovery eventually arrives at: *Who am I?*

I laughed silently at the old comic answer: *I don't know. Who's asking the question?* And there on the rain-soaked road in my soppy T-shirt, I received a unique gift such as comes most often to those who hit the pavement running with no good reason for doing so. *Who am I?* I'm a student and a teacher. I'm a parent and a child. I'm a provider and a monk. I am often lost, and I am sometimes found. I am all these things, and I am none of them. I am ripe with the contradiction of what it means to be human. Underneath all the roles and responsibilities, there's a continuity that extends outward toward infinity in all directions. It's that continuity that I long to touch, that I yearn to know. Sometimes the path is easy, sometimes it's demanding. But each time I stumble or become distracted by my roles, I get up and continue. How do I know these things? Because, in the end, I'm both the runner and the path. I leave my footprints on it, but more important, the path leaves its impression on me. And this is as it has always been, and how it will always be. It is only me that forgets it and becomes confused on the point.

I could go home and sleep. A warm, dry bed awaited.

21

Running Together

"Lord, make us instruments of your peace. Where there is hatred, let us sow love; where there is injury, pardon; where there is discord, union; where there is doubt, faith; where there is despair, hope; where there is darkness, light; where there is sadness, joy. Grant that we may not so much seek to be consoled as to console; to be understood as to understand; to be loved as to love. For it is in giving that we receive, it is in pardoning that we are pardoned, and it is in dying that we are born to eternal life. Amen."
—The Prayer of St. Francis

Although she's twelve now, and our days of running half marathons together are over, my dog Izzy has lost none of her enthusiasm. She still jumps with excitement if I even touch my running shoes or open the closet that holds her leash. Her once brown face is all gray, but when it's time to run, she still behaves just like a puppy. Chris tells Izzy to sit as she slips on her collar, but even sitting, Izzy can't stop wagging her tail, swishing the floor like a windshield wiper. Izzy and I have run the equivalent of four or five trips across the country together.

Just as I turn to load Zach in the baby jogger, he runs off down the hallway with fast little cartoon steps, laughing. A moment later, he returns with four plastic lizards and holds them up for me. "You gotta have lizards, Daddy!" I agree that lizards are good to have, and I open the front door and turn to pick him up in the same motion.

Zach is heavy like a cinder block. He's almost too big now for the baby jogger. It wasn't so long ago that he looked like a harnessed peanut as he sat in it, but he barely fits in the seat now. Time indeed flies. Soon we'll be running together, and not so long after, he'll be pushing me.

Two mourning doves perch on the telephone line in front of our house, facing each other and cooing. Izzy bounds out of the front door with Chris in tow, and the birds fly off together, wings squeaking as they rise. Tonight is date night for Chris and me. We have a window-seat reservation at Skates on the Bay, where we can watch the sunset over the Golden Gate Bridge. I'm looking forward to it.

As we walk out to the end of the driveway, the sun is breaking through the morning overcast, bathing us with its wonderful warm light. Zach's forehead, once so coarse and callused from scratching his eczema, looks soft and smooth for the first time ever. He's participating in a new drug-efficacy study, and the medication is working. For a few uncomfortable, sleepless nights, the cure seemed worse than the disease, but now the results speak for themselves, and Chris and I are hopeful. We've been told that his eczema will continue to flare up, but at least we no longer need to slather him in steroid cream to keep him comfortable, and the side effects of the steroids will no longer concern us.

"Can we go see the attack cow please, Mommy?" Zach asks, referring to a plywood black-and-white Jersey cow that one of the neighbors has attached to a fence, alongside a sign that says BEWARE OF ATTACK COW. In our family, it's become a celebrated landmark.

"Of course we can," Chris says.

With Izzy pulling Chris and me pushing Zach, our little parade begins running toward the attack cow. I'm struck by how rare and precious this moment is. How often does a man get to go running with those he loves most in the world? Each time must be savored. Just then, I stumble over my clumsy feet and Chris grabs my elbow to steady me.

In that moment, I think, *Thank God I got it right*. So many years ago, before I asked Chris to marry me, I asked myself some important questions: *Will this person help me grow spiritually? Will I help her?* And the answer came: Yes. For once in my life, I got it right the first time. First Chris, and now Zach, continue to push the boundaries of my understanding of love.

"You take good care of me, don't you?" I tell her.

"Well, I love you, and I do the best I can," she says.

I wonder what more anybody could possibly ask. I'm not a wealthy man, but I'm surrounded by riches. Before us the road stretches. We resume our run. "I love you too," I say.

22

Beginning and Ending

"Everything in the universe evolved, he said. And, for wise men, gold is the metal that evolved the furthest. Don't ask me why; I don't know why. I just know the tradition is always right. Men have never understood the words of the wise. So gold, instead of being seen as a symbol of evolution, became the basis for conflict . . . I have known true alchemists, the alchemist continued. They locked themselves in their laboratories, and tried to evolve, as gold had. And they found the Philosopher's Stone, because they understood that when something evolves, everything around that thing evolves as well." —Paulo Coelho, *The Alchemist*

It's the first spring Saturday morning that we can sit outside comfortably. Zach is playing in the sand with his trucks, and I'm sitting and enjoying a cup of coffee while Chris sweeps the patio. For a while she pushes the leaves and dirt into a little pile, then she leans over and peers into the debris. She pulls earthworms and other bugs out and puts them in the grass, then sweeps the rest of the pile into the dustbin and dumps it in the garbage. This gentleness, that doesn't even want to harm a bug, is a favorite aspect of her personality. She has just finished reading about half of the first manuscript of this book, and I've asked her what she thinks so far. As I do, I remind myself: *Good or bad, don't react. Instead, concentrate on listening to what she has to say.*

"Honestly?" Chris said.

"Yes. Don't sugarcoat it. I want to know what you really think."

"I didn't like the introduction. So much so that I think it tainted my reading of the rest of the book." She wasn't being mean, just honest, as I had asked. I thought: *My best friend and harshest critic.*

"Why?"

"Because it's just so hard to read. It's really different from the rest of the book."

"That's okay. I was trying to put a framework around what I was writing. Besides, the book is a little bit like a run. There are hard parts and easy parts. The hard parts give context to the easy ones."

She said, "You and Marc might enjoy all this esoteric stuff, but people won't like it. Nobody really wants to read the phrase *delicious inner alchemy*. If you were taking a group of runners out for the first time, you wouldn't run them up the side of a mountain, would you? I'm afraid that if you turn readers off in the introduction, they'll never read the rest of the book. You do want people to read your book, don't you?"

Ouch. "Well, of course, I want people to read the book," I said, feeling hesitant. "But this stuff has to be said. The book isn't complete without it."

"Then put it at the end. That way, when people stop reading it, they've already finished the rest of the book."

"Thanks." *I guess*. Sometimes I hate the truth.

Life sometimes gets a little unruly. This book is a lot like life. I sat down, intending to write a celebration of the running experience. I wanted to capture the feelings of unfettered joy that come with cresting a mountain, using your own power. I wanted to describe the sensation of liberation and relief that comes with the first few downhill strides that follow. I wanted to write about how running transforms lives, and provides an organizing influence that helps and heals. And I wanted to talk about running as an art—running not to get faster, but to slow down, running not to live longer, but to live more fully, running not to get away, but to come home. I wanted to capture the wit and wisdom of the people whom it's been my pleasure to run with. This book is about all of that, but it's something more.

It's about realizing that running is just one footpath through the wilderness of human experience. Some of the other trails are marriage, career, raising a child, thinking, and feeling. When I write about running, I have to write about marriage, my job, and raising Zach. I have to write about thoughts and feelings. All the trails that make up our lives intertwine and interconnect. Little wonder, then, that the book, like life, sometimes meanders in unexpected directions, becoming tangled and, yes, a little unruly.

But after a time you notice an underlying simplicity. Even though the paths of marriage, career, parenting, and running traverse different terrain, you begin to see the unmistakable pattern of trails across the landscape. A trail looks like a trail, whether it crosses a desert, cuts through a meadow, winds through a forest, traverses an ice field, or climbs over a high mountain pass. In the same way, years of running hold many of the same patterns as years of marriage or years of career. A certain unmistakable design emerges. The big, existential questions that underpin all human trails are the same: Who am I? What is my relationship to this path? What do I genuinely know about my life? Am I living it well by traveling down this particular path? A unifying reorientation occurs when we ask these questions, whenever we find ourselves lost.

Sometimes when we ask these questions, just as when we're hiking, we encounter sages, mystics, and philosophers who point us down the trail. This book tries to express my gratitude to those running mystics who pointed the way when I was lost.

Writing, like running, is a process. Writing offers the advantages of a relatively straight path through the wilderness. For a long time, my MBA-trained mind calculated the monetary value of my time, deciding that I couldn't afford the luxury of writing. But later, as I aged and the luster of career began to fade, I realized the importance of the vehicle. (Writing *is* delicious!) An inner alchemy begins the moment the trinity of author, pen, and paper sit down together. The act of writing changes all three. In the end, the pen has spilled some ink and the paper has received it. But the real magic is when the writer sits down believing he's an author, and gets up knowing he's just a pen that's being guided by a larger, unseen hand toward new insight and comprehension.

In the end, the writer understands that the real running trail he writes about, like all genuine trails through human experience, is the one that leads us to ourselves. I realized that if writing promotes this unavoidable journey, I could no longer afford the poverty of a life lived without it.

Chris once flattered me: "I never worry about you running off with another woman. I worry that you'll run off and join a Buddhist monastery." There's no Buddhism in my background, though in hectic times I have fantasized about doing just that. But it would be too easy. If becoming a monk meant ignoring the dirty dishes of daily life, it would be no different than riding the adrenaline of a high-powered career while turning my back on the quest for deeper meaning. For me, the search must occur within the context of job, relationships, community, and family, not sequestered from the world.

I'm fascinated by the moments of conflict, friction, and irritation when the ego meets the outside world and doesn't like it. (I think of ego as desire for personal gain, not just in the usual sense of acquiring money, power, and prestige, but gain also by avoidance: avoiding things deemed undesirable, such as fears and petty expectations.)

What happens when a business negotiation doesn't go as we expected? What happens in our hearts when we arrive late at the airport? What causes the irritation we feel, reading the newspaper on the couch when the dog begins barking to be let out? Do we gloss over the friction, denying that it's there? Do we even notice it? Must we suffer through these moments, or is there a better way?

There's something elemental and true in these moments, something about our own nature that we may be tempted to pave over reflexively before we've had a chance to see it clearly. And it happens many times every day. If there's such a thing as conscious living, I suspect that it begins in those moments; that we must expose them even as we try to conceal something from ourselves, to the light of our attention.

I suspect the road to self-discovery is paved with just these moments. That's why these stories fall within the context of everyday life, during business negotiations, in conversations between marriage partners, in the line at a fast-food restaurant, and while running down the trail. If we've decided to struggle to lead a genuinely spiritual life, here and now may be the best place to begin. If not here, then where? A monastery would be pleasant—or would it? I prefer to think of the postmodern world as graduate-level course work.

This book is my attempt to drill deep into the moment of friction and report what I have found. I encourage others to look at their lives and see if they can make similar discoveries. I've tried to be honest about my journey, but I must insist that you not take my word for any of what I've said. After all, a person who asks big existential questions such as *Who am I?* is implying *I might be wrong*. So I encourage you to seek for yourself. Cultivate a spirit of self-inquiry. That alone will bring meaning into your life. In my experience, self-questioning is like running—sometimes easy, sometimes hard, but the effort leaves us energized, engaged, and fulfilled.

Where Are They Now?

Shortly after the time of this book, I left RadioGear, accepting a position with a start-up company based in San Diego. I work out of my home in Walnut Creek, and can still be found on the trail running with Izzy or philosophizing with Marc.

Zach recently turned four, and begged to swim in his first meet. I wasn't so sure I wanted to expose him to competition so early in his life. But he persisted. Chris and I stood in amazement as he swam twenty-five yards using his big arms and side breathing the whole way. As I lifted him out of the pool, he looked at me through his goggles and said, "Daddy, do I get a ribbon cuz I did so good?"

"Yes Zach, you do," I said.

"Can we frame it?" He asked.

"We can," I replied.

And so it is. Chris and I watch with wonder as events unfold in front of us. We are lucky to have each other.